DIVINE FOOTPRINTS

Christ in the Old Testament

Eugene P. Kauffeld

Drawings by Sheryl Kauffeld Ertl

PUBLISHING HOUSE

Northwestern

MILWAUKEE, WISCONSIN

Library of Congress Card 82-62109
Northwestern Publishing House
3624 W. North Ave., Milwaukee, WI 53208-0902
©1983 by Northwestern Publishing House. All rights reserved
Published 1983

Printed in the United States of America
IBSN 0-8100-0148-9

*Dedicated to my wife and family
for the great support they have given me
in my ministry.*

TABLE OF CONTENTS

FOREWORD

Ever since I was a boy I have always marveled at the prophecies concerning Christ in the Old Testament. It was a never failing source of interest and delight to see how, when God gave his Word, everything in nature and in humanity had to move so that it would be fulfilled.

As I read and studied the Bible over the years, the words from the story of the two disciples on the way to Emmaus caused me to trace the "footsteps" of our Master through the Old Testament:

> Then he said unto them, O fools, and slow of heart to believe all that the prophets have spoken: Ought not Christ to have suffered these things, and to enter into his glory? And beginning at Moses and all the prophets, he expounded unto them in all the scriptures the things concerning himself. And they drew nigh unto the village, whither they went: and he made as though he would have gone further. But they constrained him, saying, Abide with us: for it is toward evening, and the day is far spent. And he went in to tarry with them. And it came to pass, as he sat at meat with them, he took bread, and blessed it, and brake, and gave to them. And their eyes were opened and they knew him; and he vanished out of their sight. And they said one to another, Did not our heart burn within us, while he talked with us by the way, and while he opened to us the scriptures? (Luke 24:25-32 KJV)

The book of Acts increased my desire to do so when it said:

> To him give all the prophets witness, that through his name whosoever believeth in him shall receive remission of sins. (Acts 10:43 KJV)

In Sunday school, parochial school, high school, college and seminary, I came to recognize more of his "footprints" but they were not as clear and connected as I felt they could and should be. Accordingly, in my Bachelor of Divinity thesis I began a study of the "Roles of Christ in the Old Testament."

Through the years of my ministry I have sought to build on this study with a study of the prophecies, the resultant concept of God among God's people in the Old Testament and the existence of the church of God in the Old Testament. I have drawn these studies together in this volume.

This book is written to show what a beautiful picture of the Savior the believers had at the time of Christ. I have deliberately avoided using much Hebrew, Greek and technical language other than some Hebrew names and terms listed below. In this way even children should be able to follow the "footprints" of the Master in the Old Testament and thus be enabled to see their Lord more clearly and fully in the New Testament. It is my hope that this will also help God's people to understand Holy Writ and to see that all of Scripture is a beautiful, connected and unified whole pointing to Christ. Such an understanding of the Bible is sadly overlooked by many of God's children today.

I pray that this volume will encourage God's people, both old and young, to walk onward in faith, joy and confidence in the "footprints" of their Master. He leads us from earth to heaven through his Word, the Bible.

* * * * * * * * * *

Some Hebrew terms will be used in this book which are commonly used in the Hebrew Bible and in Old Testament studies. They are:

Jahweh (Yah-weh, Jahwe) or Jehovah — A name pointing to God as the Covenant God, the God of Promises. In most translations this name is rendered as the LORD.

Elohim (El-o-heem) — A name indicating God as the High, the Mighty God.

Mal'akh (Mal-ach) — The Hebrew term for angel. It means messenger just as the word angel does.

Ebed (Eb-ed) Jahweh — The Hebrew term for Servant of the Lord.

Dabar (Da-bar) Elohim — The Hebrew term for the Word of God.

Chok-mah (Chok-mah) — The Hebrew term for wisdom.

Messiah — The Anointed One — Identical in meaning to the Greek word Christ, a term used to identify the hoped-for Savior and King of the Old Testament people of God.

Ruach — Spirit, Breath.

Various translations are used deliberately. The author chose that translation which he felt most fully brought out the Messianic meaning of the passage. Multi-usage was also employed to demonstrate that the message of the coming Christ is common to all the translations used. Here is a listing of the translations with their abbreviations:

An American Translation by William F. Beck — AAT

The New Berkeley Version — Ber.

The Interlinear Hebrew/Greek/English Bible by Jay Green — Gr.

King James II — KJ II

King James Version — KJV

New International Version — NIV

1. SIMEON — A BELIEVING OLD TESTAMENT JEW OF JESUS' DAY

Simeon's Great Hymn of Praise

Now there was a man in Jerusalem, Simeon by name, an upright and devout man who was looking for the consolation of Israel. The Holy Spirit was on him and it was divinely communicated to him by the Holy Spirit that he would not see death before he had seen the Lord's Christ. Moved by the Spirit he came into the temple and, when the parents brought in the child Jesus to perform the legal ritual for Him, he took Him up in his arms and thanked God, "Now let Your bond servant depart in peace, Lord, in agreement with Your word, for my eyes have seen Your salvation, which You have prepared before all the nations, a light for revelation to the Gentiles and a glory to Your people Israel." (Luke 2:25-32 Ber.)

"And behold there was a man in Jerusalem, whose name was Simeon." That is all Simeon was — a man. He was an elderly, devout, believing Jew. Yet his words of praise to his gracious God have become immortal. To this day, we, with many other Christians of the New Testament era, might do well to ask ourselves why these words remain immortal and their glory enhanced by time.

Let us look at the words. Literally translated, the first verse reads, "Master, now permit your slave to leave in peace, according to your word." In these words some significant concepts appear. The faith of the believing Israelite at the time of Christ centered in the Old Testament gospel covenant relationship with God in the coming Messiah.

The book of Genesis describes the first giving of this covenant when it says:

> And I will put enmity between you and the woman, and between your seed and her seed. He will bruise your head, and you shall bruise his heel. (Genesis 3:15 Gr.)

It was renewed with Noah and his family and then with Abraham. Finally at Mt. Sinai God beautifully set his covenant before his people Israel through Moses in the books of Exodus and Deuteronomy:

> You have seen what I did to the Egyptians, and how I bore you on eagles' wings and brought you to Myself. Now, then, if you will obey My voice indeed, and keep My covenant, then you shall be a peculiar treasure to Me above all people — for all the earth is Mine. And you shall be to Me a kingdom of priests and a holy nation. These are the words which you shall speak to the children of Israel. (Exodus 19:4-6 KJ II)

> For you are a holy people to the LORD your God. The LORD your God has chosen you to be a special people to Himself, above all people that are on the face of the earth. (Deuteronomy 7:6 KJ II)

Simeon's faith was not that of a work-righteous person, secure in the knowledge that he was a member of God's chosen people descended from Abraham and hence an heir of heaven and a little better than anyone else. Neither was there the feeling, that since he as an Israelite stood in the Old Testament law covenant relationship to God, also given to Moses at Mt. Sinai, he was thereby assured of a place in heaven. This was indeed the faith of the Pharisees and their followers. But Simeon's faith so far transcended that of the Pharisees that they can hardly be compared, except by contrast. Simeon's faith was based on God's Mosaic gospel covenant, the promise of the coming Savior. It was not based on the Mosaic law covenant. The law covenant could first of all only convict him of sin. In its ceremonial aspect it set before him God's coming sacrifice for sin. To this promised sacrifice and its result he clung by faith.

Simeon, as was mentioned, stood in the Mosaic law covenant relationship to God and he knew it. As one of God's children he adhered to God's command given in Genesis 17:

> This is My covenant, which you shall keep, between Me and you and your seed after you; every man child among you shall be circumcised. And you shall circumcise the flesh of your foreskin. And it shall be a token of the covenant between Me and you. (Genesis 17:10,11 Gr.)

However, the mere fact that he was circumcised, that he bore on his body the mark of God's people, and that he attended religious services in the temple did not make Simeon utter his beautiful confession and prayer in what we call the "Nunc Dimittis." His faith in God's gospel covenant, begun in the Garden of Eden, caused him to utter his beautiful confession.

Note how he begins his prayer. "Master, now permit your slave, your bondman, to leave this world in peace." Simeon was fully conscious of the concept, which to the Christian today is so dynamic, namely, that believers in Christ are slaves, bondmen of God. We know the reason we are bondmen of God is that he has bought us to be his own with the precious blood of his Son, Jesus Christ. The

Jews applied the term slave, or bondman, only to one who had been purchased to become the personal property or chattel of another. Slavery had always been a part of their history. Scripture declares that Abraham, their ancestor, had owned slaves:

> And she said to Abraham, Drive away this slave-girl and her son; for the son of this slave-girl shall not inherit with my son, with Isaac. (Genesis 21:10 Gr.)

The practice of slavery was limited by God in the civil or political aspect of the Mosaic law:

> When you buy a Hebrew slave, he shall serve six years; and in the seventh he shall go out free for nothing. (Exodus 21:2 Gr.)

To Simeon being a slave of God was truly a marvelous blessing and the basis of a feeling of boundless security. He stood before God as a purchased slave, asking only to be permitted to leave this world in peace. He knew and stood firmly in the true covenant relationship to God. He well knew God's words which stated:

> There is not a righteous man on earth who does what is right and never sins. (Ecclesiastes 7:20 NIV)

The Source of Simeon's Hope

Although he was a sinner, Simeon knew he could hope in God's mercy and forgiveness. This hope rested not in any merit on Simeon's part, for he was but a slave of God. No, his hope rested solely in the promised Messiah, his Redeemer, his Salvation. What God told him through the prophet Isaiah he believed:

> Behold, My servant shall rule wisely; He shall be exalted and extolled and be very high. (Isaiah 52:13 Gr.)

Therefore I will divide Him a portion with the great, and He shall divide the spoil with the strong; because He has poured out His soul to death; and He was counted among the transgressors; and He bore the sin of many and made intercession for the transgressors. (Isaiah 53:12 KJ II)

In this faith and confidence Simeon asked for a peaceful death, a release from this sinful world, and salvation at his Master's hands.

Simeon had often and earnestly prayed that his Master would send the Messiah. We are told that this event was something for which he had long been waiting. The Lord had revealed to Simeon that he would not die until he had seen the Savior for whose advent he had prayed so earnestly (Luke 2:26). Now he stood in the temple of God, holding in his arms that answer to his prayers. His heart was filled with joy, awe and gratitude. And from his happy heart came the prayer, "Master, now permit your slave to leave in peace, because my eyes have seen your salvation." This infant is he of whom the prophets wrote; this is he through whom salvation is to come to the world; this is he for whom I have prayed and waited; this infant is none other than the promised Messiah, the Salvation of God incarnate. He will deliver all from eternal death. This grace has been granted me, that my eyes have been privileged to see him!

So Simeon must have thought as he held the baby Jesus. This was the climax of his long life, and he burst into a song of praise to his Savior and God: "My eyes have seen your salvation which you have prepared before the face of all people." He believed what God had said to the coming Savior through prophets such as Isaiah:

> It is too light a thing that you should be My Servant, to raise up the tribes of Jacob and to restore the preserved of Israel; I will make you a light to the nations that My Salvation may reach to the end of the earth. (Isaiah 49:6 Ber.)

For Simeon, a Jew, this was a tremendous and meaningful statement. He was in effect saying that God had sent the Messiah as the salvation of all people, not only the Jews. This infant was to be made known to the entire world. God had prepared Jesus for his task with the special intention that he and his work of salvation should be of public and universal concern among all nations. Through him, salvation was to be offered to all people, releasing them from the curse of eternal death. Such was the faith of this Jewish saint. He saw in Christ not a Jewish Savior or national hero, but a universal Savior sent by God to save all mankind.

Simeon brings out this idea in the beautiful closing stanza of his song of praise, "My eyes have seen Your Salvation which You have prepared before all the nations, a light for revelation to the Gentiles and a glory to Your people Israel." The purpose of God in sending Christ was, then, that all the world might be enlightened by him, who is the Light of Life, and in whom there is no darkness. He came from heaven to shed the rays of eternal life and the light of eternal day upon the entire race of mankind, which dwelt in the darkness of eternal death and eternal night. He was sent to be Simeon's Light, your Light, my Light and the Light of all the world, that whoever would be enlightened by Christ Jesus might have the Light of Eternal Life blazing within him. This was the primary purpose of the Savior's coming.

Moreover, while he was saving man, he would be bringing the people of God their most glorious moment. As God declared through the prophet Zechariah:

> In that day Jehovah shall defend around the inhabitants of Jerusalem. And it will be, he who is feeble among them in that day shall be like David; and the house of David shall be like God, as the Angel of Jehovah before them. (Zechariah 12:8 Gr.)

The fact that the Jews chose to reject Jesus as the Messiah or Savior did not change what God said. Jesus was still their Glory. After his death and resurrection, he would remain the Glory of the Jews in a threefold sense. He would be their Glory in that he was their way to eternal glory. He would be their Glory in that for all time people of all nations would concede that the most glorious period in history was unfolded in the Jewish land of Palestine during the time Jesus was on earth. He would be their Glory in that people of all nations would concede that the most glorious personage in history was a Jew named Jesus, for he was the incarnate Son of God, the Savior and Redeemer of the world.

This, then, was Simeon, a humble believer, a sinner who trusted in God for his salvation through the promised Messiah. This was Simeon, a devout Jew, who gloried in the fact that his Savior and Way to eternal life was also to serve as the way to eternal life for all mankind, not only the Jews. He possessed the basic earmarks of a modern Christian, a knowledge of his sin, a deep faith and belief that God's salvation was for the entire world, a positive conviction that since Christ was the God-sent Savior of the entire world, he was also his personal Savior. This gave Simeon the sure hope that through faith in his Savior, eternal life with God was now waiting for him beyond death, as Moses had declared when he said:

> O Lord, Thou hast been our home in successive generations. (Psalm 90:1 Ber.)

The question remains: If Simeon had such a faith, where did he get such a clear picture of Christ and God's plan of salvation? After all, the first books of the New Testament would not be written for another fifty years after Simeon's great declaration of faith. The source of his faith had to be found in the Old Testament sacred writings, considered by the faithful Jews of his time to be the Scriptures wherein God had revealed his salvation to men. By faith Simeon had listened to the words God spoke through the prophet Isaiah:

> "Come, all you who are thirsty, come to the waters; and you who have no money, come, buy and eat! Come, buy wine and milk without money and without cost. Why spend money on what is not bread, and your labor on what does not satisfy? Listen, listen to me, and eat what is good, and your soul will delight in the richest of fare. Give ear and come to me; hear me, that your soul may live. I will make an everlasting covenant with you, my unfailing kindnesses promised to David. See, I have made him a witness to the peoples, a leader and commander of the peoples. Surely you will summon nations you know not, and nations that do not know you will hasten to you,

because of the Lord your God, the Holy One of Israel, for he has endowed you with splendor."

Seek the Lord while he may be found; call on him while he is near. Let the wicked forsake his way and the evil man his thoughts. (Isaiah 55:1-7 NIV)

Simeon had searched and found. He had thirsted for the water of life. He had found the eternal fountain of God's mercy and grace to a sinful and fallen mankind. Let us, like Simeon, look into the Old Testament Word of God and see the Messiah, the Christ, the Savior he knew and loved so well.

2. THE OLD TESTAMENT GOSPEL COVENANT

The First Promise

It is not the purpose of the author to debate the existence of God, for this is undeniable to any person who thinks clearly, objectively and positively. Matter, the cosmos and life cannot come from nothing. They had to be created by God. Anyone who denies this and the existence of God is following a man-made negative faith or religion. Such a person is pronouncing and making his religion the greatest "no" that can be pronounced: "no" to God and his works.

It is rather our purpose to show what God says to man in the Bible about his Son, Jesus, the promised Messiah and Savior of the world. The wondrous history of Jesus does not begin in Bethlehem, but it begins already in the Garden of Eden with the creation of the world and man.

God created Adam and Eve on the sixth day of creation. He placed them in the Garden of Eden. Scripture says of this:

> And God said, Let Us make man in Our image, according to Our likeness; and let them rule over fish of the sea, and over birds of the heavens, and over cattle, and over all the earth, and over every creeping thing that is creeping on

the earth. And God created man in His image; in the image of God He created him; He created them male and female. And God blessed them. And God said to them, Be fruitful and multiply and fill the earth, and subdue it; and rule over fish of the sea, and over birds of the air, and over every creeping thing on the earth. And God said, See, I have given you every plant seeding seed which is on the face of all the earth, and every tree in which is the fruit of a tree seeding seed; it shall be food to you, and to every animal of the earth, and to every bird of the air, and to every creeping thing on the earth, in which is the breath of life; every green plant is for food. And it was so. And God saw everything that He had made; and, behold, it was very good! And there was evening and there was morning the sixth day. (Genesis 1:26-31 Gr.)

And Jehovah God planted a garden in Eden, to the east, and He put the man whom He had formed there. And out of the ground Jehovah God caused every tree that is pleasant to the sight and good for food to grow. The tree of life also was in the midst of the garden, and the tree of knowledge of good and evil. (Genesis 2:8,9 Gr.)

The description of the location of the Garden of Eden in the Bible indicates that it was in the area of the source of the Tigris and Euphrates Rivers:

And a river went out of Eden to water the garden, and from there it was divided and became four heads. The name of the first is Pishon; that is it which surrounds all the land of Havilah, where the gold is; and the gold of that land is good; there is bdellium and the onyx stone. And the name of the second river is Gihon; that is it which surrounds the whole land of Cush. And the name of the third river is Hiddekel; that is it which goes east of Assyria. And the fourth river is Euphrates. (Genesis 2:10-14 Gr.)

The world was now in a state of perfection and harmony with God, since Adam and Eve had not yet disobeyed God and broken the harmony and perfection that existed.

At this time the Bible describes the condition of Adam and Eve as being in "the image of God":

> And God said, Let Us make man in Our image, according to Our likeness; and let them rule over fish of the sea, and over birds of the heavens, and over cattle, and over all the earth, and over every creeping thing that is creeping on the earth. And God created man in His image; in the image of God He created him; He created them male and female. (Genesis 1:26,27 Gr.)

The image of God does not refer to man's physical appearance since God is a Spirit and has no form. Rather it refers to the fact that Adam and Eve were perfect or holy and knew God and his will. No greater human beings ever lived than Adam and Eve. They were the crowning masterpiece of creation, made to be God's children, his son and daughter, perfect in every detail.

It is fascinating to note that Adam and Eve were different from both animals and angels:

> And Jehovah God formed the man, dust from the ground, and breathed into his nostrils the breath of life; and man became a living soul. (Genesis 2:7 Gr.)

Animals are only physical creatures. Angels are only spiritual creatures created to serve God and man. Man was created to be a spiritual being with a physical body. Because there were two parts to man, we say he was dichotomous. Moreover, he was created so wondrously that he could live consciously, apart from his body, in his spiritual self which is called his soul. The marvelous way in which man was created shows itself in that after the Fall God delivered man from life on a sin-cursed earth through the separation of the body and soul in temporal death.

When God first placed man into the Garden of Eden he gave him one command, not to eat of the fruit of "the tree of knowledge of good and evil":

> And Jehovah God took the man and put him into the garden of Eden to work it and keep it. And Jehovah God commanded the man saying, You may freely eat of every tree in the garden; but of the tree of knowledge of good and evil you may not eat, for in the day that you eat of it, dying you shall die. (Genesis 2:15-17 Gr.)

This tree was special in that through its presence God called upon man to honor and obey his word. God clearly stated what would happen if man ate of it, saying, "In the day that thou eatest thereof, thou shalt surely die." The tree then would amply fulfill its name if man disobeyed, for evil would come to man in the form of death —temporal, spiritual and eternal death. If they remained obedient, good would be their lot. They would continue to live a holy and blissful life before God as his created children.

While God was creating this physical universe, he also created spiritual messengers whom we call angels. These great, mighty and holy beings were to serve God and man. Some, however, under the leadership of Satan, who was one of the leading angels of heaven, chose to disobey God. As a result God expelled them from heaven and created a place of eternal torment for them as their abode called hell:

> For . . . God spared not the angels that sinned, but cast them down to hell, and delivered them into chains of darkness, to be reserved unto judgment. (2 Peter 2:4 KJV)
>
> Then shall he say also unto them on the left hand, Depart from me, ye cursed, into everlasting fire, prepared for the devil and his angels. (Matthew 25:41 KJV)
>
> And angels who did not keep their own original state, and left their own dwellingplace, He keeps in everlasting chains under darkness to the judgment of the great Day. (Jude 6 KJ II)

Satan, in turn, decided to destroy God's world. Using a snake, he spoke to Adam and Eve and tempted them to sin by inducing them to eat of the tree of the knowledge of good and evil:

> And the serpent was crafty above every animal of the field which Jehovah God had made. And he said to the woman, Is it true that God has said, You shall not eat from any tree of the garden? And the woman said to the serpent, We may eat of the fruit of the trees of the garden, but of the fruit of the tree which is in the middle of the garden God has said, You shall not eat of it, nor shall you touch it, lest you die. And the serpent said to the woman, Dying you shall not die, for God knows that in the day you eat of it, your eyes shall be opened and you shall be as God, knowing good and evil. And the woman saw that the tree was good for food, and that it was pleasant to the eyes, and that the tree was desirable to make wise, and she took of its fruit and ate; and she also gave to her husband with her, and he ate. And the eyes of both of them were opened, and they knew that they were naked, and they sewed leaves of the fig-tree and made girdles for themselves. And they heard the sound of Jehovah God walking up and

down in the garden at the breeze of the day. And the man and his wife hid themselves from the face of Jehovah God in the middle of the trees of the garden. And Jehovah God called to the man and said to him, Where are you? And he said, I have heard Your sound in the garden, and I was afraid, for I am naked, and I hid myself. And He said, Who told you that you were naked? Have you eaten of the tree of which I have commanded you not to eat? And the man said, The woman whom You gave to be with me, she has given to me of the tree, and I ate. And Jehovah God said to the woman, What is this you have done? And the woman said, The serpent deceived me and I ate. (Genesis 3:1-13 Gr.)

When they ate of the forbidden fruit death passed upon Adam and Eve. They died temporally, spiritually and eternally. Death now was a part of man's existence in this world. Man had sinned. He had transgressed God's command. Because temporal death had become a part of human life, man's magnificent body would now die. He was also dead spiritually, separated from God by sin and subject to eternal damnation in hell, Satan's abode. Man had died because of his disobedience, as God had foretold. In perfect justice God could have sent every human being to hell and not one would have been able to say that God was being unjust.

But rather than dealing with man in perfect justice alone, God chose to deal with man in grace, mercy and love:

And Jehovah God said to the serpent, Because you have done this, you are cursed above all beasts, and above every animal of the field. On your belly you shall go, and you shall eat dust all the days of your life. And I will put enmity between you and the woman, and between your seed and her seed. He will bruise your head, and you shall bruise his heel. He said to the woman, I will greatly increase your sorrow and your conception; you shall bear children in sorrow, and your desire shall be toward your husband, and he shall rule over you. And to the man He said, Because you have listened to the voice of your wife and have eaten of the tree about which I commanded you saying, You shall not eat from it, the ground shall be cursed because of you; in sorrow you shall eat of it all the days of your life. And it shall bring forth thorns and thistles for you; and you shall eat the plant of the field. By the sweat of your face you shall eat bread until you return to the ground; for out of it you have been taken, for you are dust, and to dust you shall return. And the man called his wife's name Eve; and she became the mother of all living. And Jehovah God made coats of skin for the man and his wife and clothed them. And Jehovah God said, Behold! The man has become as one of Us, to know good and evil. And now, lest he put forth his hand and take also from the tree of life, and eat and live forever — therefore Jehovah God sent him out of the Garden of Eden to till the ground out of which he was taken. And He drove the man out; and He placed at the east of the Garden of Eden the cherubim, and the flaming sword whirling around to guard the way of the tree of life. (Genesis 3:14-24 Gr.)

God summoned all involved in this tragedy and laid upon each a judgment. The snake was reduced from the most intelligent form of creature life to one of the lowest. It would crawl in the dirt and be feared and loathed:

And Jehovah God said to the serpent, Because you have done this, you are cursed above all beasts, and above every animal of the field. On your belly you shall go, and you shall eat dust all the days of your life. (Genesis 3:14 Gr.)

27

The judgment on Adam changed the face and character of the entire world:

> And to the man He said, Because you have listened to the voice of your wife and have eaten of the tree about which I commanded you, saying, You shall not eat from it, the ground shall be cursed because of you; in sorrow you shall eat of it all the days of your life. And it shall bring forth thorns and thistles for you; and you shall eat the plant of the field. By the sweat of your face you shall eat bread until you return to the ground; for out of it you have been taken, for you are dust, and to dust you shall return. (Genesis 3:17-19 Gr.)

No longer would man live in a friendly, harmonious and productive world, but he would have to labor in a world that opposed him. Later we note that the animal world also turned on man, for God in cautioning Cain of his sin uses the picture of an animal crouching at the door. This was something that Adam and his family undoubtedly came to know well:

> If you do well, is there not acceptance? And if you do not do well, sin is crouching at the door; and its desire is toward you, and you shall rule over it. (Genesis 4:7 Gr.)

Eve had been instrumental in bringing mankind under the yoke of sin. After the fall her submission to her husband would often be a painful burden and a bitter dependency:

> He said to the woman, I will greatly increase your sorrow and your conception; you shall bear children in sorrow, and your desire shall be toward your husband, and he shall rule over you. (Genesis 3:16 Gr.)

In his curse on Satan, God in effect nullified what Satan

had done. He promised that there would be enmity or a struggle between Satan's followers among men and the Seed of Eve. It is most significant to note that the word here used for Seed is singular and points to the Savior. It speaks of one of Eve's desendents who in his struggle with Satan he would be victorious, crushing Satan's head. Nevertheless, in destroying Satan, God's promised Seed would have to suffer, for his heel would be crushed:

> And I will put enmity between you and the woman, and between your seed and her seed. He will bruise your head, and you shall bruise his heel. (Genesis 3:15 Gr.)

In these words we find the first promise of a coming Savior. This is the gospel covenant of God with man, the promise by which the Lord bound himself to redeem and save all mankind. In this covenant we can see God's tremendous love and mercy toward man.

Having made this gospel promise, God showed further mercy to man. He made clothes of animal skins for Adam and Eve. This showed man that he was free to use the animal kingdom for the support of his life. God then expelled Adam and Eve from the Garden and sealed its entrance with cherubim or angels and a flaming sword. Being outside the Garden, Adam and Eve would no longer be able to eat of the other wondrous tree in the Garden, the Tree of Life. Had they eaten of that tree after sinning, they would have lived forever in sin. Now they could live out their lives in faith in the promise of the coming Savior. Then they could leave their sinful, mortal bodies and sin-cursed world behind through temporal death and live forever with God in heaven, first in soul, and after Judgment Day in glorified body and soul. One cannot help wondering how often Adam and Eve came and stood outside the Garden, bitterly regretting their sin and longing for that life of harmony with God which once had been theirs.

Judgment and Grace

Everything had changed with the coming of sin. Nothing on earth was perfect anymore. The actions of Adam and Eve toward each other were no longer constantly harmonious. The animals and insects were no longer friendly and obedient. Even the plants and the ground would not respond as they once had. The effect of sin was vividly felt and clearly seen. How often they must have remembered God's early words in the Garden, "In the day that thou eatest thereof thou shalt surely die" (Genesis 2:17 KJV). Now they knew death. They could see it at work in themselves and in the world.

The full scope of the misery and woe their transgression would bring upon the earth was something they could not foresee. But before many years had gone by, they received a foretaste of it when their oldest son, Cain, refused to worship God in faith, killed Abel in a jealous rage and then left them and the worship of God entirely. In Cain's children all the evils of sin flowered. Through their influence the world became more and more evil until God described man as having evil thoughts continuously and the world as full of violence and evil.

Man became atheistic. He became godless and lived a life of godlessness and evil. God in justice declared that he would destroy the world. He granted man 120 years of grace. During this time God directed Noah, a believer, to build an ark. When the time of grace was over and mankind remained impenitent and unbelieving, God destroyed the world with a flood, saving only Noah and his family, one pair of each unclean animal and seven pairs of each clean animal:

> You shall take to yourself every clean animal by sevens, male and female; and from the animal that is not clean, two male and female; and of the fowl of the heavens by sevens, male and female; to keep alive seed upon the face of all the earth. (Genesis 7:2,3 Gr.)

This judgment of God for sin was never to be forgotten. It is recorded in the history of nations all over the globe. Strangely enough, though recorded in history, it has been relegated by modern man to the area of mythology and fable. Once again today sin has become rampant, violence and immorality are a way of life. Once again godlessness is everywhere to be found. Scripture declares that the last days will be like the days of Noah. Our age has become so today:

> "When the Son of Man comes, it will be like the time of Noah. In the days before the flood, they were eating and drinking, and men and women were marrying till the day *Noah went into the ark.*" (Matthew 24:37 AAT)

At this time in history we, as God's people, need to lift our eyes and pray to God for deliverance through salvation in Christ. Isaiah voices the feelings which should be in our hearts as God's children of today when he prays for deliverance and salvation in his own evil day. He refers to

God's coming down on Mt. Sinai and says for us and for himself:

> Oh, that you would rend the heavens and come down, that the mountains would tremble before you! As when fire sets twigs ablaze and causes water to boil, come down to make your name known to your enemies and cause the nations to quake before you! For when you did awesome things that we did not expect, you came down, and the mountains trembled before you. Since ancient times no one has heard, no ear has perceived, no eye has seen any God besides you, who acts on behalf of those who wait for him. You come to the help of those who gladly do right, who remember your ways. But when we continued to sin against them, you were angry. How then can we be saved? All of us have become like one who is unclean, and all our righteous acts are like filthy rags; we all shrivel up like a leaf, and like the wind our sins sweep us away. No one calls on your name or strives to lay hold of you; for you have hidden your face from us and made us waste away because of our sins.
>
> Yet, O LORD, you are our Father. We are the clay, you are the potter; we are all the work of your hand. Do not be angry beyond measure, O LORD; do not remember our sins forever. Oh, look upon us, we pray, for we are all your people. Your sacred cities have become a desert; even Zion is a desert, Jerusalem a desolation. Our holy and glorious temple, where our fathers praised you, has been burned with fire, and all that we treasured lies in ruins. After all this, O LORD, will you hold yourself back? Will you keep silent and punish us beyond measure? (Isaiah 64:1-12 NIV)

Would that God would tear apart the sky! Would that he would come down to judge! Would that the mountains might melt and flow away before the flame of his glory.

God did this once before when he appeared on Mt. Sinai. Then, as it were, the mountains flowed down before him. Still man keeps forgetting. He is sinful and thus does not grasp what God has in store for those who faithfully wait for him. God comes in love and mercy to those who believe and walk in his ways.

Yet we are all as an unclean thing and all our righteousnesses are as filthy rags. Our very age is evil. Nevertheless, God remains our Father. He is the potter; we are the clay. May we be mindful of his just judgments! And may his forgiveness, his mercy, his grace rest upon us, because we have no other help, no other hope. God's grace was and is centered in the promised Savior. In the Christ, the Messiah, the world was and is offered salvation.

This gracious offer from God is called simply "the covenant" in the Old Testament. In this covenant Jesus is pictured in breathtakingly beautiful pictures which grow in beauty and clarity as the Old Testament approaches the New Testament age. St. Peter refers to this proclamation by the prophets and its fulfillment in Christ, saying:

> "Moses said: *The Lord our God will raise one of your people to be a Prophet to you like me. Listen to everything He tells you. And destroy anyone among the people who will not listen to that Prophet.* Samuel and all the other prophets after him, as many as have spoken, told about these days. You are the heirs of the prophets and of the covenant God made with our fathers when He said to Abraham: *And in your Descendant all the people on earth will be blessed.* Now that God has given His Servant, He sent Him first to you to bless you by turning everyone of you from your wicked ways." (Acts 3:22-26 AAT)

The words of the Old and New Testament gospel covenant are remarkably similar and extremely beautiful in their summary forms. The Old Testament summary of the gospel covenant between God and his people is found in Exodus and Deuteronomy:

> You have seen what I did to the Egyptians, and how I bore you on eagles' wings and brought you to Myself. Now, then, if you will obey My voice indeed, and keep My covenant, then you shall be a peculiar treasure to Me above all people — for all the earth is Mine. And you shall be to Me a kingdom of priests and a holy nation. These are the words which you shall speak to the children of Israel. (Exodus 19:4-6 KJ II)

> For you are a holy people to the LORD your God. The LORD your God has chosen you to be a special people to Himself, above all people that are on the face of the earth. (Deuteronomy 7:6 KJ II)

The New Testament summary of the covenant relationship of God with his people is found in 1 Peter:

> But you are a chosen generation, a royal priesthood, a holy nation, a people who belong to God, so that you might show forth the praise of Him who called you out of darkness into His wonderful light. (1 Peter 2:9 KJ II)

In reality there is no difference between the gospel covenant relationship of God to his Old Testament people and his New Testament people. The Old Testament believers looked forward to Christ and were saved. The New Testament believers look back to Christ and are saved. Both sought heaven. May we by grace ever remain God's covenant people in time and in eternity!

3. OLD TESTAMENT PICTURES OF THE MESSIAH

The Messiah as the Promised Seed

From Adam to Noah

As we saw in the last chapter, the first mention of the coming Messiah or Savior is in Genesis 3:15. Here he is referred to as the "Seed" of the woman. Speaking to Satan, God said:

> And I will put enmity between you and the woman, and between your seed and her seed. He will bruise your head, and you shall bruise his heel. (Genesis 3:15 Gr.)

It is interesting to note that in telling man about the coming Savior the first time, God used the concept of the "Seed." In this basic concept the entire general picture of the life and work of the Messiah was portrayed. It is worth pointing out again that the word for "Seed" here refers to one Descendent, namely the Savior.

To see the full beauty of this passage, one needs to keep in mind that after they had sinned Adam and Eve knew they no longer possessed the holy relationship they once had. They also knew that they were spiritually condemned before God. The former close and loving relationship was gone. Death had touched them and they were powerless to reconcile themselves to God. This is

35

Christ as the Seed

The Seed

why they had tried to hide from God in the Garden.

One other thing which needs to be noted is that after they fell into sin Adam and Eve were only one step removed from perfection. Even after the Fall they were able to live more than 900 years. Compared to Adam and Eve, we of today are simpletons in understanding and weaklings in strength. Knowing their abilities, God spoke to them in words which they could and would understand. They had to understand, for their salvation depended on it. Having far greater capabilities than we, they undoubtedly understood and accepted the Messianic content of this passage much more fully and readily than we do. In their situation they would also have desired an immediate redemption and reconciliation with God.

When God pledged that there would be warfare or enmity between the followers of Satan and the Seed of Eve, they grasped God's meaning and believed it. When God added that the Coming One or Seed would crush the head of the snake, Adam and Eve understood this to mean that he would destroy Satan who had destroyed them through the snake. When God further stated that this Seed would have his heel crushed by the snake, they understood he would suffer in his battle for them but would emerge victorious. In this promise they understood that the enmity between God and man created through sin was now over. By faith in the promise they again belonged to God who would send the Seed as the Savior. After their earthly lives were over, they would again be reunited in person with God, their Creator and Lord.

That Adam and Eve believed this can be seen in the

births and naming of their first two sons. When the first son was born Eve said, "I have gotten a man, the LORD" (Genesis 4:1 AAT). (Editor's note: This verse can also be translated: "With the help of the Lord I have brought forth a man" [NIV]. Whether Adam and Eve actually thought Cain was the promised Seed is open to discussion. As the author points out in the following paragraphs, whatever lofty ideas they might have had about Cain were brought to earth by his behavior.)

She and Adam believed him to be the promised Savior and accordingly named him Cain, which means "Possession." In his name they were stating that they possessed the Savior. Abel's birth and naming again indicated their faith, for the name means, "Useless, Vain, Needless." In his name they were possibly stating that in Cain they had all they needed according to God's promise, Abel was really not necessary. They could not know or imagine the untold years that would pass under sin as time progressed and the untold misery and heartache their act in the Garden would bring to the earth and its creatures, including man.

A preview of the enormous consequences of their sin was given them in their children. Adam and Eve faithfully taught them about God and the coming Savior. They taught them to worship God with sacrifices. In spite of their teaching and example, Cain chose to turn away from God. After being rejected by God in his sacrifice, he became angry and killed Abel, who had been accepted by God in his sacrifice. Instead of confessing his sin, Cain resented God's rebuke and judgment. He took his sister-wife and left his parents' home with its worship of God and built a home and life of his own. His descendants became the unbelievers and the ungodly people of the earth. They intermarried with the godly who followed Adam and Seth, a later son, in the worship of God. As time went on the godly people grew less numerous until finally there were only a very few left out of perhaps billions on earth. Finally man became so wicked that God decided to destroy the earth with a flood.

God gave to eight people, Noah, his wife, his sons (Shem, Ham and Japheth) and their wives the task of building an ark for the preservation of life on the earth. They were granted 120 years, which also became a time of grace for the world. The world did not repent in spite of Noah's warnings and at the end of the 120 years God destroyed it in the Flood.

It must have been a tremendous comfort to Noah and his family that already before the Flood God established his covenant with Noah, namely, the promise of the coming Savior which had been given to Adam and Eve in the Garden of Eden. As we have noted, this was recorded in Genesis 3:15.

Noah was now to be the bearer of the promise. How often he and his family must have remembered this grace of God during their confinement on the ark. We read of the establishment of this covenant with Noah in Genesis 6:18:

> But I will establish My covenant with you. And you shall come into the ark — you and your sons and your wife and your sons' wives with you. (KJ II)

When Noah and his family finally left the ark, the sinful human race was beginning for the second time. It is significant to note that just as God sent Adam and Eve into the world with the promise of the coming Savior, so he now sent Noah and his family into the world with the assurance that his gospel covenant still held. Nothing would ever cause it to be withdrawn. What God had pledged before the Flood still held and would continue to hold.

In addition, God promised that no world-wide flood would ever again occur. The rainbow was to serve as a reminder to man of God's never failing promises — redemption in the Seed and unfailing mercy toward the physical world. God's words in this respect are very beautiful. He said to Noah:

> And surely the blood of your lives will I require. At the hand of every animal I will require it, and at the hand of man. At the hand of every man's brother I will require the life of man. Whoever sheds man's blood, his blood shall be shed by man, for God made man in the image of God. And you be fruitful and multiply. Bring out abundantly in the earth and increase in it. And God spoke to Noah, and to his sons with him, saying, Behold! I, even I, establish My covenant with you, and with your seed after you —and with every living creature that is with you — from all that go out from the ark, to every animal of the earth. And I will establish My covenant with you. Neither shall all flesh be cut off any more by the waters of a flood. Neither shall there any more be a flood to destroy the earth. And God said, This is the token of the covenant which I make between Me and you and every living creature that is with you, for everlasting generations: I set my bow in the cloud. And it shall be a token of a covenant

between Me and the earth. And when I bring a cloud over the earth, the bow shall be seen in the cloud. And I will remember My covenant which is between Me and you and every living creature of all flesh. And the waters shall no more become a flood to destroy all flesh. And the bow shall be in the cloud. And I will look upon it that I may remember the everlasting covenant between God and every living creature of all flesh that is on the earth. And God said to Noah, This is the token of the covenant which I have established between Me and all flesh that is on the earth. (Genesis 9:5-17 KJ II)

In these words God's gospel covenant was re-established with mankind through Noah and his family. They were also given a guarantee of mercy to the physical world and its creatures.

From Abraham to David

Mankind soon showed, however, that its main concern was with the physical life. Human relationships became more important than the spiritual life and the coming Savior. God's command to spread out over the earth was deliberately disobeyed. After about 300 years, instead of spreading out over the earth as they had been commanded to do, mankind decided to build a huge temple tower which would occupy them, keep them together, and cause them to be remembered by future generations. Since at this time all men were of one race and spoke one language, they were united in this goal. God dealt with them in a gentle but devastating fashion. He suddenly divided mankind into various languages and peoples. The result was that men could no longer live together in unity and peace and they spread out over the earth.

About 1900 B.C. God called a man from the descendants of Shem, named Abram, later known as Abraham, from Ur of the Chaldees, to be the bearer of the promise of the Savior. He was to be the ancestor and father of the nation from whom the Savior or "Seed" would be born. Several passages in the book of Genesis point to Abraham as the one in whom the whole world would be blessed. This worldwide blessing would be centered in his coming Descendant or "Seed":

> And I will bless those who bless you, and curse the one who despises you; and in you shall all families of the earth be blessed. (Genesis 12:3 Gr.)

> And Jahweh said, Shall I hide from Abraham the thing which I do, when Abraham shall surely become a great and powerful nation, and all the nations of the earth shall be blessed in him? (Genesis 18:17,18 Gr.)

> And in your Seed shall all the nations of the earth be blessed, because you have obeyed My voice. (Genesis 22:18 KJ II)

In the book of Acts Peter refers to this last passage and applies it to Christ, saying:

> "You are the heirs of the prophets and of the covenant God made with our fathers when He said to Abraham: *And in your Descendant all the people on earth will be blessed.* Now that God has given His Servant, He sent Him first to you to bless you by turning every one of you from your wicked ways." (Acts 3:25,26 AAT)

Abraham, according to God's promise, was given a son. He named him Isaac, which means "Laughter," thereby indicating that Isaac would be the bringer of joy to his parents and to the world. We might say that in Isaac

God's joy for men had begun, for in him the building of the Messianic nation, the cradle of the Savior, had its beginning. Isaac's son, Jacob, became the father of the nation from whom the Savior would be born. God renamed Jacob "Israel," meaning "Prince of God" or "Warrior of God," thereby indicating that he and his descendants would be known as God's children on earth, royal children, the children of heaven's King. "Israel" became the name of God's Messianic people, their badge of honor as it were.

They were the people of the Savior. From the sons of Jacob came the twelve tribes which made up the nation of Israel. One of them was chosen as the tribe of the Savior. It was the tribe of Judah.

God forged these tribes into his Messianic people during 400 years of slavery in Egypt. In their deliverance from Egypt he made them to be a type or picture of the Savior who was later called from Egypt, as we see from the books of Hosea and Matthew:

> When Israel was a boy, I loved him and *I called My son out of Egypt.* (Hosea 11:1 AAT)
>
> Joseph got up at night, took the little Child [Jesus] and His mother, and went to Egypt. He stayed there till Herod died. In this way what the Lord said through the prophet was to come true: *I called My Son from Egypt.* (Matthew 2:14,15 AAT)

Many years after Israel's exodus from Egypt, the prophet Nathan told King David that the "Seed" or the Savior would be descended from him and would establish an eternal kingdom. David's "Seed" would be the Son of

God, and God would cause him to suffer for the sins of mankind:

> And when your days are fulfilled, and you shall sleep with your fathers, I will set up your seed after you, who shall come out of your bowels. And I will make his kingdom sure. He shall build a house for My name, and I will establish the throne of his kingdom forever. I will be his Father, and he shall be My son. If he commits iniquity, I will chasten him with the rod of men, and with the stripes of the children of men. (2 Samuel 7:12-14 KJ II)

One of the Psalms speaks of this when it says:

> You said, "I have made a covenant with my chosen one, I have sworn to David my servant, 'I will establish your line forever and make your throne firm through all generations.' "

> "I will also appoint him my firstborn, the most exalted of the kings of earth. I will maintain my love to him forever, and my covenant with him will never fail. I will establish his line forever, his throne as long as the heavens endure."

> "I will not violate my covenant or alter what my lips have uttered. Once for all, I have sworn by my holiness — and I will not lie to David — that his line will continue forever and his throne endure before me like the sun; it will be established forever like the moon, the faithful witness in the sky." (Psalm 89:3,4,27-29,34-37 NIV)

David also rejoiced in this blessing and often praised God for his love and goodness and mercy. He sings of the coming Savior and points to his coming as a definite fact and event of the future. David writes:

> The Lord says to my Lord: "Sit at my right hand until I make your enemies a footstool for your feet." The Lord will extend your mighty scepter from Zion; rule in the midst of your enemies. (Psalm 110:1,2 NIV)

He who would be sent by God was David's Lord. He would come and establish the kingdom of God. Jesus, in speaking of this passage, refers it to the Messiah and hence to himself:

> But the Pharisees being gathered together, Jesus asked them, saying, What do you think about the Christ? Whose son is He? They said to Him, The son of David. He said to them, How then does David in Spirit call Him Lord, saying, "The Lord said to my Lord, Sit on My right hand until I place Your enemies as a footstool for Your feet"? Then if David calls Him Lord, how is He his son? (Matthew 22:41-45 KJ II)

The coming of the Savior was the source of comfort, strength, peace and hope to God's people. David expressed this beautifully, especially in the beloved Twenty-third Psalm, "The Lord is my shepherd." Although it does not name "the Lord" as the Messiah, this Psalm shows the Good Shepherd to be the one who loves, feeds, and conducts his sheep to the eternal sheepfold of heaven. Jesus identifies himself with Psalm 23 when he calls himself the Good Shepherd:

> I am the Good Shepherd! The Good Shepherd lays down His life for the sheep. (John 10:11 KJ II)

When death silenced the voice of David, the "Sweet Singer of Israel," the spiritual decline of Israel began and eventually led to its material and political decline. This has ever been and will ever be the pattern of nations and peoples. When God ceases to be a reality for man, then man degenerates. In his degeneracy, man reverts to animalistic standards and ways. Such living is always the beginning of the end of a people or nation. So it also came to be for Israel.

The Prophets

Though under David's son, Solomon, the nation reached its peak of luxury, glory and peace, it also became the time when Solomon, in spite of all his God-given wisdom, led the nation into idolatry. This caused an obscuring of Israel's mission on earth as God's Messianic people, the cradle and herald of the coming Savior. As a result, God stated that he would divide the nation into two parts, the one having ten tribes and the other part having two tribes. The larger part became the Northern Kingdom and was called Israel. The smaller part became the Southern Kingdom and was called Judah. Its formation and naming was a reminder to all of the Messianic role of Judah and the coming Hope of God's people and of the world.

The people of the Northern Kingdom permitted themselves to be led into calf worship by their first king, Jeroboam. They followed their subsequent kings into wholesale idolatry. God sent prophet after prophet to warn them of their sins and to point them to the Savior. Scripture tells us that all the prophets pointed to the forgiveness which was to be found in the coming Savior:

> All the prophets witness to Him, that through His name everyone that believes on Him receives remission of sins.
> (Acts 10:43 KJ II)

The people refused to hear. The result was that the Northern Kingdom was destroyed. This destruction took place when the ten tribes were carried off into captivity by the Assyrian nation under King Sargon in 722 B.C.

While this was transpiring in Israel in the north, little Judah in the south was slowly but surely becoming like its big brother, Israel. Judah, however, had some good kings and by working with the prophets these men managed to slow the growth of idolatry and its attendant vice and immorality.

Yet the course was set and slowly but surely Judah degenerated spiritually. In its latter days God sent the great prophet Isaiah to his people. Isaiah pointed to the coming Savior more clearly than any other Old Testament prophet and urged the people to repent and believe. He also foretold the fall of Judah, as well as its captivity and return.

In a day of national crisis brought on by an alliance of Israel and Syria against Judah, Isaiah urged Judah's evil king, Ahaz, to trust in God. Speaking through his prophet Isaiah, the Lord even offered to provide a miraculous sign of His grace and blessing. When Ahaz hypocritically refused the sign, Isaiah gave to the king a sign from God in a beautiful Messianic prophecy:

> Therefore the Lord Himself shall give you a sign, Behold, the virgin shall be with child and shall bring forth a son; and she shall call His name Immanuel. He shall eat curds and honey until He knows to refuse the evil and choose the good. For before the boy shall know to refuse the evil and choose the good, the land that you hate will be forsaken before both her kings. (Isaiah 7:14-16 Gr.)

Here Ahaz is told that instead of being destroyed by the alliance of Syria and Israel, Judah would survive. As God had foretold, the Messiah or Savior would be born from the tribe of Judah. His birth would be a wonderful happening in that he would be born of a virgin. He would be wonderful himself in that he would be Immanuel, "God with us," God and man in one person.

The time of his birth would be a time when the fortunes of Judah would be very low. His food would be butter and honey, the food of the desert dweller, the shepherd and the poor. By the time of his birth, the sins of the house of David and of Judah would have ravaged the nation and reduced it to poverty. Only by God's grace would it live on to produce the promised Savior. Before the Messiah's childhood the enemies which Ahaz dreaded would be gone.

In another prophecy Isaiah sees the child born. As a human child he is born into the world, but as divine, he is God's own Son. Being divine, he would have the right and power to reign over all. He would be Wonderful. He would be the God-Man. Isaiah exclaims:

> For to us a Child is born, to us a Son is given; the government shall be upon His shoulder, and His name shall be called Wonderful, Counselor, Mighty God, Everlasting Father, Prince of Peace. (Isaiah 9:6 Ber.)

In chapter 11 of Isaiah the Messiah is seen as coming from the line of Jesse (the father of King David), thus designating him as the Messianic King foretold of old:

> A shoot will come up from the stump of Jesse; from his roots a Branch will bear fruit. (Isaiah 11:1 NIV)

Having seen the promised Seed in prophetic vision,

Isaiah declares that he would be the Branch, the tree of life for all.

Again in chapter 11, Isaiah pictures the wondrous child as the one who would gather together the people of God, not only from Judah but also from the gentiles throughout the world:

> In that day the Root of Jesse will stand as a banner for the peoples; the nations will rally to him, and his place of rest will be glorious. (Isaiah 11:10 NIV)

Though Isaiah pictured the coming Savior so vividly and beautifully, the people did not care. They turned more and more to idolatry and evil. Finally the time of grace for Judah came to an end and God began to bring upon Judah what he had foretold.

As the end of Judah drew near, the great prophet Jeremiah was given the task of warning the people. As he spoke of God's impending judgment and the imminent destruction of Judah, he bade them lift up their hearts and eyes by faith to believe and to see the fulfillment of God's promise of salvation in the Son of David, the righteous and holy Branch who would be the tree of life for all:

> Behold, the days come, says the LORD, that I will raise to David a righteous Branch, and a King shall reign and act wisely, and shall do judgment and justice in the earth. In his days Judah shall be saved, and Israel shall dwell safely. And this is His name by which He shall be called, THE LORD OUR RIGHTEOUSNESS. (Jeremiah 23:5,6 KJ II)

In the Messiah would be centered all judgment, justice and salvation. In him God's people would dwell safely forever. He would be called the "Lord our Righteousness" because through him God's righteousness would rest upon sinful mankind.

Years passed. The seventy years of captivity under the Babylonians came and went. Under Cyrus, the Persian king, a remnant returned to rebuild the Promised Land in order that God's promise of the birth of the Messiah might be fulfilled. At this time God spoke through the prophet Zechariah:

> "'Listen, O high priest Joshua and your associates seated before you, who are men symbolic of things to come: I am going to bring my servant, the Branch. See, the stone I have set in front of Joshua! There are seven eyes on that one stone, and I will engrave an inscription on it,' says the Lord Almighty, 'and I will remove the sin of this land in a single day. In that day each of you will invite his neighbor to sit under his vine and fig tree,' declares the Lord Almighty." (Zechariah 3:8-10 NIV)

In these words, God through the prophet Zechariah pointed his people to the coming Messiah and the spiritual glory, pardon and peace which would be found in him and his kingdom. Joshua as the high priest and his fellow priests were symbols of the great High Priest to come, the Messiah. Joshua in his name and office of high priest typified the Savior. His name, Joshua, came from the same Hebrew word as Jesus. The name means "the Lord saves." He is told to listen to what God would tell him. He and his fellow priests are to look at what God was about to set before them. As they looked, a wondrous Stone was set before them. It had seven eyes. These eyes were symbolic of the sevenfold spirit of God which would dwell within the Stone. On that Stone God would place an inscription and in one day an atonement would be made for the sins of all. This pardon and redemption would lead to peace and joy, a peace and joy that would never end.

Again in Zechariah, God says through his prophet:

> Thus speaketh the LORD of hosts, saying, Behold the man whose name is The BRANCH; and he shall grow up out of his place and he shall build the temple of the LORD. Even he shall build the temple of the Lord; and he shall bear the glory, and shall sit and rule upon his throne; and he shall be a priest upon his throne: and the counsel of peace shall be between them both. (Zechariah 6:12,13 KJV)

A golden future lay ahead of God's people in the coming Branch, the promised Seed, the Seed of David, the tender Shoot from the root of Jesse. He would come and bring eternal salvation to all. He would be both High Priest and King and would build God's temple, the church. He would be its High Priest. He would be its King. His priesthood and his reign would spread over the whole earth. In his priesthood all men would find the sacrifice necessary for peace with God; and in his kingly reign all men would find security, shelter, safety, life and peace unending. In him all men would find eternal life in heaven.

The Branch was coming. The promised Seed would come as a tree of life for all. He would come and save his people. What a joyous hope belonged to the people of God!

Christ as Prophet

The Messiah as the Promised Prophet

Prophets, Priests, Kings

In an expanding and ever more beautiful way, God painted the portrait of the coming Savior. No physical description was given, but by using concepts, ideas and types, God prepared a picture of the Savior which was easily recognized with the eyes of faith.

Not only was the image of the coming Messiah etched in the words of the Old Testament, but the very organization of the nation of Israel held the coming Redeemer before the people. They were a covenant people and their lives were to reflect this. This covenant had as its foundation the promise of the redemptive coming of the Savior in Genesis 3:15. Apart from this initial base, God's relationship to his people cannot be understood. In an unbroken line this redemptive promise or covenant continued till the coming of the Savior. From the time of the Savior it will continue to the end of time. This was and is the basic covenant of God with man. Its central theme was and is Christ.

It was the sacred duty of the leaders to hold before the people of God this gospel covenant. The messages of the *prophets*, the sacrifices and teachings of the *priests*, and the rules of the *kings* were to be centered in this covenant. If we are to understand the roles of Christ as Prophet, Priest and King, we must first review just what these offices were. For Christ was the climax of each office; each one pointed to him.

In this section we shall discuss the role of the prophet. The prophets were the primary defenders and heralds of the covenant. They were messengers of God, men who proclaimed a message which was not their own. As *the* Prophet above all others, Christ insisted that the Father had sent him and that he carried out the Father's will in all he did.

The background of the gospel covenant is found in Adam and Eve and what took place in the Garden of Eden. The hope of a suffering but victorious Savior contained in the first gospel promise sustained the believers before the Flood and brought them to eternal life. However, so rudimentary was the law in man's heart after the Fall and so sinful was man, that mankind degenerated to the point where God had to destroy the whole human race in the Flood, with the exception of Noah and his family.

We have already noted how immediately after the Flood, God renewed his gospel covenant with Noah and his family.

God now began to prepare from Shem (one of Noah's sons) and from Abraham, a descendant of Shem, the nation which was to be the cradle of the Savior and to be the herald of God's salvation to the world. He forged this special nation in 400 years of slavery in Egypt, where its only hope lay in God's gospel covenant and in his promise of deliverance given to Abraham:

> And He said to Abram, You must surely know that your seed shall be a stranger in a land that is not theirs. And

they shall serve them. And they shall afflict them four hundred years. And also I will judge that nation whom they shall serve. And afterward they shall come out with great substance. And you shall go to your fathers in peace. You shall be buried in a good old age. (Genesis 15:13-15 KJ II)

When the time was come God delivered them from their bondage and led them to the Promised Land. Even at this time the Lord Jesus, as the great Mal'akh Jahweh or Angel of the Lord, acted as the Savior of his people. He led them and shielded them, for he was in the pillar of cloud and fire which guided them throughout their forty years of wandering between Egypt and the Promised Land. When the years of wandering were over, God settled his people in Palestine, the land bridge of the world of that day. They stood at the crossroads of the world where all could see and hear them. God did not put them there to become rich or powerful, but to show the world the gospel covenant of God in the Messiah, the coming Savior. Thus the nation of Israel was to glorify God before the whole earth.

On their way to the Promised Land, God led his people to Mt. Sinai. There he renewed the promise of the coming Savior. In Exodus and Deuteronomy we read:

You have seen what I did to the Egyptians, and how I bore you on eagles' wings and brought you to Myself. Now, then, if you will obey My voice indeed, and keep My covenant, then you shall be a peculiar treasure to Me above all people — for all the earth is Mine. And you shall be to Me a kingdom of priests and a holy nation. These are the words which you shall speak to the children of Israel. (Exodus 19:4-6 KJ II)

> For you are a holy people to the LORD your God. The
> LORD your God has chosen you to be a special people to
> Himself, above all people that are on the face of the earth.
> (Deuteronomy 7:6 KJ II)

Again we point out that this identical gospel covenant relationship to God is granted to the New Testament believer:

> But ye are a chosen generation, a royal priesthood, an
> holy nation, a peculiar people; that ye should show forth
> the praises of him who hath called you out of darkness
> into his marvelous light. (1 Peter 2:9 KJV)

God's gospel covenant has never changed. The Old Testament believers were saved by looking *forward* to Christ's coming, the New Testament believers are saved by looking *back* to Christ's coming. The relationship to God in Christ remains the same.

It was not until after the people had God's gracious gospel covenant at Mt. Sinai that God gave the Ten Commandments, as a summary of his moral law. After declaring this law orally, the Lord inscribed it on two tablets of stone. Now man again fully possessed the moral law. It was in written form. It was clear. It set before God's people and the world the perfect standard by which God requires all mankind to live for all time. Anything contrary or less was a sin and would bring on men God's judgment. As God gave the Ten Commandments in written form, he also set before his people what is called the ceremonial and political or civil law. Together with the moral law these laws separated God's people from the heathen and united them in their faith and hope.

The ceremonial law was the religious law of God's Old Testament people. It was basically a sacrificial law and served as a shadow cast by the coming cross which pointed to Christ. As long as God's people walked in this shadow or shade of God's grace they would not step into the blazing sun of the moral law. Every sacrifice was a type of the coming Savior. We might say it was an audio-visual presentation of the coming Messiah. God's people well knew that the blood of bulls, goats, sheep, doves and pigeons could not remove human sin. These sacrifices were rather a constant reminder of a higher sacrifice to come — that of the Messiah. As they sacrificed, meditated and walked in faith, they would unerringly be led to Christ. As they watched and listened to the priest, the priest became for them a type of the great High Priest to come in his role as Mediator, Sacrificer and Sacrifice.

The political law established Israel as a people governed by God. Although the early theocratic form of government in which it was ruled directly by God gave way to a monarchy, the nation was still supposed to be guided by God through the prophets and priests. The kings were supposed to rule as the "Lord's anointed." Each king was a type of the King who would come from the tribe of Judah and from the family of David.

Moses and the Prophets

When at Sinai the people pleaded for Moses to function as the mouthpiece of God for them, the prophetic office of the Old Testament came into being. Every prophet also became a type of the great Prophet to come, the Messiah or Savior. Thus in the offices of prophet, priest and king the Old Testament believers were granted a beautiful threefold portrait of their coming Lord. That this was not something unknown to the Old Testament believers can easily be seen in the prophecies concerning these offices.

Peter said of this message of the prophets:

> Samuel and all the other prophets after him, as many as have spoken, told about these days. (Acts 3:24 AAT)

Moses declared:

> Jehovah your God shall raise up to you a Prophet from among you, of your brothers, One like me; to Him you shall listen. (Deuteronomy 18:15 Gr.)

As the Israelites beheld Moses and listened to him, they were all to keep in mind that a greater Prophet was yet to come. He would come to God's people not only as a man but as their great Deliverer. This coming Prophet would be the One who would be the culmination of the prophets' line. His voice was to be heard by all.

Peter referred to this prophecy and applied it to Christ and said:

> "Moses said: *The Lord our God will raise one of your people to be a Prophet to you like me. Listen to everything He tells you.*" (Acts 3:22 AAT)

God said of this:

> I will raise them up a Prophet from among their brothers, like you. And I will put My words in His mouth. And He shall speak to them all that I shall command Him. (Deuteronomy 18:18 KJ II)

Here Moses was held up as a type of the coming

Prophet. God pointed out that the coming Prophet's role would be like that of Moses, only greater. Whatever God would give him to say or do he would carry out. It is interesting to note that the coming Prophet would be divinely sent and would be a separate person in the Godhead. What an honor it was to be an Old Testament prophet! You were a picture of the Great One and it was your joy to instruct as he would, to guide as he would, to love as he would, to protect as he would. The prophets were the torch bearers, the lights, the heralds of the coming Lord.

The prophet Isaiah looked forward to his coming Master and said:

> Nevertheless, there will be no more gloom for those who were in distress. In the past he humbled the land of Zebulun and the land of Naphtali, but in the future he will honor Galilee of the Gentiles, by the way of the sea, along the Jordan — The people walking in the darkness have seen a great light; on those living in the land of the shadow of death a light has dawned. (Isaiah 9:1,2 NIV)

Looking forward over the years he saw a time of glory for the area about the Sea of Galilee. Where death and darkness would reign because of the Assyrians, there the light of life would be seen. From there it would shine and its rays would reach out to lighten the way of God's people. It was a beautiful picture of the coming Messiah or Prophet and pinpointed the main area of his ministry on earth.

A prophet was to be filled with God's Spirit. Isaiah again pointed to his coming Lord and said:

> And the Spirit of Jehovah shall rest on Him; the spirit of wisdom and understanding, the spirit of counsel and power; the spirit of knowledge and of the fear of Jehovah. (Isaiah 11:2 Gr.)

The coming Prophet would be anointed in a way different from human prophets. On human prophets an anointing oil would be poured. To each human prophet God gave different gifts. One would be given a gentle spirit, another an overpowering spirit. Though each human prophet was bound by the limits of his humanity this would not be true of the Coming One. On him the Spirit of God would rest in all its fullness. In him would rest divine wisdom and understanding. His would be divine counsel and might. In him would rest divine knowledge and fear or devotion to God. Such a person could not be a mere man. He would have to be God and man — just as Isaiah pictured this great Prophet with his divine and human nature.

In the latter chapters of this book, Isaiah again set before his people the coming Prophet. In fact, Isaiah relayed a message from the coming Prophet himself, in which he describes his special task:

> The Spirit of the Lord GOD is upon me; because the LORD hath anointed me to preach good tidings unto the meek; he hath sent me to bind up the brokenhearted, to proclaim liberty to the captives, and the opening of the prison to them that are bound; to proclaim the acceptable year of the LORD, and the day of vengeance of our God; to comfort all that mourn; to appoint unto them that mourn in Zion, to give unto them beauty for ashes, the oil of joy for mourning, the garment of praise for the spirit of

heaviness; that they might be called trees of righteousness, the planting of the LORD, that he might be glorified. (Isaiah 61:1-3 KJV)

In these words we note that the coming Prophet would be anointed with the Spirit of God. The Spirit here spoken of is the Holy Spirit. Thus in this passage we have another instance in which there is set before us a plurality of persons in the Godhead. The coming Prophet or Messiah is speaking. The Holy Spirit rests upon him. The Lord anoints or selects the Prophet and sends him.

He would come to bind up the broken-hearted, to comfort and strengthen them. He would come to proclaim liberty to the captives of sin, death and hell, to release those who are locked and chained in the dungeons of sin. He would come to proclaim the time of God's grace and love, the acceptable year, the time when God will wreak vengeance on Satan. He would come to dry the tears of those who are crying because of sin. He would come to give them beauty in place of their ashes of penitence and grief. He would come to give them the oil of joy for their grief. He would come to clothe them with everlasting gratitude in heaven, in place of despair and weariness and the hopelessness of sin and death and hell. He would come to do this so that God's people might be called "trees of righteousness," those who stand uprightly and live righteous lives. He would come that they might be the seedlings of God, that God might be glorified in them.

Even though the coming Prophet would be sent on such a glorious mission by God, those who bore the name of

God's people would reject him. The prophet Zechariah pointed to this when he said:

> Then I took my staff called Favor and broke it, revoking the covenant I had made with all the nations. It was revoked on that day, and so the afflicted of the flock who were watching me knew it was the word of the LORD. I told them, "If you think it best, give me my pay; but if not, keep it." So they paid me thirty pieces of silver. And the LORD said to me, "Throw it to the potter" — the handsome price at which they priced me! So I took the thirty pieces of silver and threw them into the house of the LORD to the potter. Then I broke my second staff called Union, breaking the brotherhood between Judah and Israel. (Zechariah 11:10-14 NIV)

The prophet, at God's command, had broken his staff, Beauty or Favor, which had been a symbolic representation of the favor and blessing of God resting upon his people. Now that it was broken, it pointed to a time when God's favor or blessing would no longer rest on the Hebrew people.

The prophet then asked the people to set a value on him. They gave him thirty pieces of silver, the price of a dead slave. It was a scornful act and indicated their anger and their rejection of the prophet and his message.

God told Zechariah to throw the money to the potter who was working in the temple. In doing so, God was rejecting and reproving the scorn of the people. This then led to the final act of the prophet, the breaking of his other staff, Union. This staff had stood for the unity of God's people. By despising God's prophet, God's people had lost God's favor and had become a broken and a divided people.

Through this incident in the life of his prophet, God was pointing to that which would take place in the Prophet of prophets, the Messiah. He would be scorned and despised. He would be valued as a dead slave, thirty pieces of silver being given for him. He would be rejected. By rejecting him, Israel would lose the blessing of being God's people. They would become a broken, divided people. In valuing their Lord as a dead slave they would become dead as God's people.

God again pointed to the division of his people when he said:

> Arise, O sword, over my shepherd, and over the man who is my neighbor, is the saying of Jehovah of hosts: smite the shepherd, that the sheep may be scattered; and I will bring back my hand over the little ones. (Zechariah 13:7 Keil and Delitzsch)

The Lord pointed to the sword descending on his representative, his Shepherd. As a result the sheep, the followers of the Shepherd, would be scattered. Yet even in this scattering the hand of God would rest over the defenseless and the helpless. The day would come when the One God sent would be killed and his followers scattered. But in that day God's protecting hand would still be over his children.

Christ as Priest

The Messiah as the Promised Priest

The Priestly Office

Through the prophetic office of the Old Testament God's people were shown that the Savior would come as the mouthpiece of God. He would teach and preach and show them the way to eternal life.

The priestly office opened up another Messianic dimension. The priests of God's people were from the tribe of Levi and were descended from Aaron. The remainder of the Levites were divided into the Kohathites, the Merarites and the Gershonites. These served in the temple. The Kohathites came to specialize in music; the others cleaned, served as doorkeepers, etc. The priests were regarded as representatives or ambassadors of God. They were mediators between God and man. They offered sacrifices for man to God. They led the people in worship, instructed them, guided them and sought to bring them to hope in God for forgiveness and eternal life. Every sacrifice was a reminder to them and the people that the great High Priest would come to suffer and die for them. He would combine in himself the dual role of both Priest and Sacrifice. In him all who believed would find pardon, peace and eternal life.

Though the office of priest was high and though it portrayed the coming great High Priest, all the earthly priests were not faithful. Some dishonored their high station and misused the office. In the early days of Samuel this sad condition existed. A man named Eli was the high priest and his sons, Hophni and Phinehas, also functioned as priests. These sons were so evil that Scripture describes them as worthless. They were a disgrace to the priesthood, but Eli was too weak to do anything. God sent a prophet to him and denounced him, foretelling the judgment that would befall him and his sons. Then God foretold the coming of the great High Priest saying:

> And I will raise up a faithful priest to Myself, one who shall do according to that which is in My heart and in My mind. And I will build him a sure house, and he shall walk before My anointed forever. (1 Samuel 2:35 KJ II)

The book of Psalms takes up the theme of this coming great High Priest or Messiah. In beautiful words the psalmists recount the enmity of the people. They foretell some of the events of the Messianic day, and portray the Messiah sacrificing himself.

David the great psalmist pictures him betrayed by a friend:

> Even My friend whom I trusted, *who ate My food, gives Me a hard kick.* (Psalm 41:9 AAT)

He foretells that false witnesses will arise against him:

> Don't give me up to the will of my enemies, because they appear against me as false witnesses, breathing out accusations of crime. (Psalm 27:12 AAT)

> Men get up and accuse me of crime; they ask me questions I can't answer. (Psalm 35:11 AAT)

David goes further and beautifully depicts the Messiah's suffering and death, saying:

My God, my God, why have you forsaken me? Why are you so far from saving me, so far from the words of my groaning? O my God, I cry out by day, but you do not answer, by night, and am not silent.

Yet you are enthroned as the Holy One; you are the praise of Israel. In you our fathers put their trust; they trusted and you delivered them. They cried to you and were saved; in you they trusted and were not disappointed.

But I am a worm and not a man, scorned by men and despised by the people. All who see me mock me; they hurl insults, shaking their heads; "He trusts in the LORD; let the LORD rescue him. Let him deliver him, since he delights in him."

Yet you brought me out of the womb; you made me trust in you even at my mother's breast. From birth I was cast upon you; from my mother's womb you have been my God. Do not be far from me, for trouble is near and there is no one to help.

Many bulls surround me; strong bulls of Bashan encircle me. Roaring lions tearing their prey open their mouths wide against me. I am poured out like water, and all my bones are out of joint. My heart has turned to wax; it has melted away within me. My strength is dried up like a potsherd, and my tongue sticks to the roof of my mouth; you lay me in the dust of death. Dogs have surrounded me; a band of evil men has encircled me, they have pierced my hands and my feet. I can count all my bones; people stare and gloat over me. They divide my garments among them and cast lots for my clothing.

But you, O LORD, be not far off; O my Strength, come quickly to help me. Deliver my life from the sword, my precious life from the power of the dogs. Rescue me from the mouth of the lions; save me from the horns of the wild oxen. (Psalm 22:1-21 NIV)

The beginning words of this section of Holy Writ are words which Jesus spoke when on the cross. He describes the loneliness of being left with human sin by God the Father. He pictures the hateful actions of the people and his terrific thirst. With his arms stretched out above his head, his ribs are so visible they seem to be staring at him. He watches as they divide his clothing and cast lots for his robe. He asks the Father to watch over him and help him.

David continues this beautiful Psalm:

> I will declare your name to my brothers; in the congregation I will praise you. You who fear the LORD, praise him! All you descendants of Jacob, honor him! Revere him, all you descendants of Israel! For he has not despised or disdained the suffering of the afflicted one; he has not hidden his face from him but has listened to his cry for help.
>
> From you comes my praise in the great assembly; before those who fear you will I fulfill my vows. The poor will eat and be satisfied; they who seek the Lord will praise him —may your hearts live forever! All the ends of the earth will remember and turn to the LORD, and all the families of the nations will bow down before him, for dominion belongs to the LORD and he rules over the nations.
>
> All the rich of the earth will feast and worship; all who go down to the dust will kneel before him — those who cannot keep themselves alive. Posterity will serve him; future generations will be told about the Lord. They will proclaim his righteousness to a people yet unborn — for he has done it. (Psalm 22:22-31 NIV)

In this latter portion of the Psalm, the great High Priest tells how the Father will answer his prayer for help. He speaks of the worldwide proclamation of his work of atonement, and he prophesies that it will be a blessing to the world until the end of time.

Psalm 69 again takes up the theme of the suffering and death of the great High Priest. The writer says by inspiration:

> Reproach has broken my heart, and I am full of heaviness; and I looked for some to mourn with me, but there was none; and for comforters, but I found none. They also gave me gall for my food; and in my thirst they gave me vinegar to drink. (Psalm 69:20,21 KJ II)

Here the High Priest is again speaking of his feelings at his death. He finds no comforters and has only vinegar or sour wine and gall to drink. In spite of his love, he is confronted by adversaries.

He turns to prayer:

> For my love they are my enemies, but I give myself to prayer. (Psalm 109:4 KJ II)

The psalmist records the certainty of the eternal priesthood of the Messiah, saying:

> Jehovah has sworn and will not repent: You are a priest forever after the order of Melchizedek. (Psalm 110:4 Gr.)

The coming Messiah would forever be a Priest like Melchizedek of Abraham's day. The name Melchizedek means "the King of Righteousness." Melchizedek was king of the city of Salem, "the city of Peace." In later years this city came to be known as Jerusalem. Mystery surrounds Melchizedek. Abraham recognized him as a priest of the true God and gave him his offering of a tithe. While Abraham scorned the King of Sodom, he accepted the blessing of Melchizedek:

Then Melchizedek king of Salem brought out bread and wine. He was priest of God Most High, and he blessed Abram, saying, "Blessed be Abram by God Most High, Creator of heaven and earth. And blessed be God Most High, who delivered your enemies into your hand." Then Abram gave him a tenth of everything.

The king of Sodom said to Abram, "Give me the people and keep the goods for yourself."

But Abram said to the king of Sodom, "I have raised my hand to the LORD, God Most High, Creator of heaven and earth, and have taken an oath that I will accept nothing belonging to you, not even a thread or the thong of a sandal, so that you will never be able to say, 'I made Abram rich.' I will accept nothing but what my men have eaten and the share that belongs to the men who went with me — to Aner, Eshcol and Mamre. Let them have their share." (Genesis 14:18-24 NIV)

Nobody knows who Melchizedek really was. Some have felt that he was Shem, who could still have been alive at this time and have migrated into Canaan. Whatever the case may be, Melchizedek is held up as a type of Christ in Scripture. His name alone makes him a beautiful picture of the Messiah. When you add to this the fact that he had no predecessor or successor in the priestly office he becomes a most unusual and beautiful type of Christ.

Sacrifice and Temple

Since, as Scripture declares, the priesthood of the great High Priest symbolized by Melchizedek will last forever, his sacrifice of himself at the hands of the earthly priesthood is not in vain. Through it God will cause his cathedral, the holy Christian church, to be built on him as its Cornerstone. The psalmist speaks of this when he says:

The Stone which the builders rejected has become the Head of the corner. (Psalm 118:22 Gr.)

Isaiah picks up the theme of God's great temple or cathedral, which would be built upon the Messiah:

> And in the last days the mountain of the LORD's house shall be established in the top of the mountains, and shall be exalted above the hills, and all nations shall flow into it. And many people shall go and say, Come, and let us go up to the mountain of the LORD, to the house of the God of Jacob. And He will teach us of His ways, and we will walk in His paths. For out of Zion shall go forth the Law, and the word of the LORD from Jerusalem. And He shall judge among the nations and shall rebuke many people; and they shall beat their swords into plowshares, and their spears into pruning-hooks. Nation shall not lift up sword against nation, neither shall they learn war any more. (Isaiah 2:2-4 KJ II)

Here Isaiah pictures how the message of the Savior and his reign in the hearts of men will span the entire world. People from every land will be drawn to this temple to worship the Savior. Eventually the end of the world will come followed by eternal, perfect, universal peace and prosperity. Then no sin or trial will affect God's people, for they will worship him forever in the temple of heaven.

Isaiah elsewhere speaks of the Cornerstone on which God's great church or cathedral would be built:

> Therefore thus says the Lord GOD, Behold, I place in Zion a Stone for a foundation, a tried Stone, a precious Cornerstone, a sure Foundation — he who believes shall not flee. (Isaiah 28:16 KJ II)

God declares that he is going to lay a special Cornerstone under his church. Its special nature is indicated by a

71

successive series of descriptions of the Cornerstone in a rising crescendo. God is going to put down a Stone. As we see the name "Stone" applied to the coming Savior, it is interesting to note that one of the proper names for God in the Old Testament is "Rock." The Cornerstone will be a divine Stone. This Stone will be tested, as it atones for the sin of the world. It will be a precious Stone, none other than God's own Son. It is the sure foundation for God's cathedral, the certain entry into heaven for all. Whoever trusts in this Stone need not fear or despair.

To relieve all doubts as to the coming of the Redeemer, God guarantees his coming through Isaiah, saying:

> And the Redeemer shall come to Zion, and to those who turn from transgression in Jacob, says the LORD. (Isaiah 59:20 KJ II)

The Messiah is coming as the Redeemer. He has purchased all mankind in the greatest sacrifice of all time, himself. He is going to come to Zion, his earthly temple in Jerusalem. To all who would believe on him, he will come not as the Redeemer of the earthly Zion of Jerusalem, but as the Redeemer who will open to penitent sinners the Zion of heaven.

After king Solomon's reign, Zion stood for the temple of Solomon in the minds of the people. It was one of the wonders of the ancient world. The people were proud of its glory and renown. It was the center of the nation and its worship. It was in a sense a symbol of the beauty and glory of heaven. When it was destroyed, it seemed that the glory of God's people was gone. When the remnant returned from the captivity in Babylon and began to rebuild the temple, some cried because this second temple which was to replace Solomon's temple was far inferior to the original in beauty and glory. But God through the prophet Haggai showed his people its coming glory:

> And I will shake all the nations; and the desire of the nations shall come. And I will fill this house with glory, says Jehovah of hosts. (Haggai 2:7 Gr.)

God here assured his people that this second temple would have a special glory, a glory greater than that of Solomon's. The great High Priest, the Messiah himself, would walk its courtyards and halls.

In order to prepare for his coming, God would shake the world. Ancient history vividly shows how he did this. He shook down the nations around the Mediterranean until at the time of Christ there was only one empire, the Roman Empire. The entire Mediterranean world at this time was in one political unit. It is significant to note that it has not been so since. There was one common world language, Greek. There was one system of law and order, Roman. All countries around the Mediterranean were joined by highways leading from one to the other. All shared one time of peace, a forty-year period of world peace. This period of peace was so unusual that it has been given a name, the Pax Romana — "the Roman Peace."

God declared that after such a shaking had taken place, the true Desire of all nations, the Messiah, the High Priest, would come to his temple in Jerusalem. In his coming he would bring to the temple its finest and most glorious hour.

Christ as King

The New Testament

God
the Father

The Old Testament

The Messiah as the Promised King

"Shiloh"

We have noted that in many ways God sought to teach his people about the coming Savior. He used familiar concepts and through them created an image of the Messiah. Another one of these was the concept of the Messiah as King. The earthly king was the head of the nation. The entire nation came under his rule. All were to obey him. The King in turn was to protect and safeguard God's people, and serve as an example for them. Thus it would have been strange if God had not used the office of king to describe the coming Savior. He did so in great beauty.

God began the idea of the Savior as King when Jacob prophesied:

> The scepter shall not depart from Judah, nor a Lawgiver from between his feet, until Shiloh come. And the gathering of the people shall be to Him. (Genesis 49:10 KJ II)

In these words God stated that the reign of Judah over God's people would continue until Shiloh would come. Shiloh is definitely pictured as the coming Messiah. The word "Shiloh" has one of two meanings. The one, basing the word "Shiloh" on a root which means to ask, says this refers to the Desired One or Asked For One. The other and more common meaning takes the word "Shiloh" from a root which indicates to be at peace or rest; hence the word has come to mean the Prince of Peace or the Bringer of Peace.

According to this prophecy there would always be a Judean king on the Judean throne until the Messiah would appear. In other words, when there was no longer a Judean king on the Judean throne, the Messiah would come. All God's people were to gather to him. He would be the climax, the magnet, the center of God's people, the one who would bring God's peace to the world.

This prophecy should be taken together with the prophecy of Isaac to his son Esau:

> And by your sword you shall live and shall serve your brother. And when you shall have the dominion, you shall break his yoke from off your neck. (Genesis 27:40 KJ II)

When these two prophecies are put together, the exact time of the Savior is pinpointed as are the events which would take place. Isaac here stated that the day would come when Esau would rule over Jacob. In other words, the day would come when an Edomite, a descendant of Esau, would occupy the Judean throne. In an amazing fulfillment, this took place in Herod the Great who occupied the Judean throne when Christ was born. Herod was an Edomite.

Having established the dynasty of Judah, and having foretold the coming of the Shiloh from Judah, God expanded the concept of the Messiah as King when he spoke through Balaam:

> I see Him but not now; I observe Him but not nearby. A Star shall come up out of Jacob, a Scepter shall rise out of Israel, which shall crush Moab from one end to the other and destroy all the children of Sheth. (Numbers 24:17 Ber.)

God enabled Balaam to look into the future and see the coming King. He saw him rise out of history like a star, glorious and shining. As a King, he would rise out of the nation of Israel. Dominion and power would belong to him and he would destroy the enemies of the people of God.

This prophecy became a source of great comfort to God's people of all ages. Their King would rule over the earth and destroy his people's foes. Thus no harm would come to the people of God of any age and finally they would live with their King in glory and peace, since their enemies would be no more.

The Psalms

The concept of the Messiah as King is frequently referred to by the Old Testament writers. A number of Psalms take up this theme. For example, Psalm 2 states:

> Why do the people rage,
> And the nations imagine a vain thing?!
> The kings of the earth rise in rebellion,
> And the rulers take counsel together —
> Against Jahve and against His Anointed.
> "Up! let us burst their bands asunder,
> And cast away their cords from us!"
> He who is enthroned in the heavens laughs,
> The Lord hath them in derision.
> Then shall He speak to them in His wrath,
> And thunder them down in His hot displeasure:
> "— And yet have I set My King
> Upon Zion, My holy hill."
> (Psalm 2:1-6 Keil and Delitzsch)

Here God speaks to those who refuse to submit to his

reign and the reign of his Anointed One. In scorn and derision God laughs at their impudence and declares that in spite of man's rebellion he has set his King, the Messiah, upon the throne of Zion. Man's words and intentions are hollow. What God has determined is all that really matters. His will determines what is to be, not man's will. The Messiah will come. He will rule. All who accept him will be blessed.

The Messiah now speaks and repeats the divine decree concerning himself and his coming:

> I will speak concerning a decree!
> Jahve saith unto me: Thou are My Son,
> This day have I begotten Thee.
> Demand of Me, and I will give Thee the nations for
>   Thine inheritance,
> And the ends of the earth for Thy possession.
> Thou shalt break them with an iron sceptre,
> Like a potter's vessel shalt Thou dash them in pieces.
> (Psalm 2:7-9 Keil and Delitzsch)

The coming King points out that he is the only begotten Son of God (Jahweh) and that all judgment has been placed into his hands. None are exempt from his reign and power. He therefore admonishes all rulers and men, saying:

> And now, O ye kings, be wise,
> Be admonished, ye judges of the earth!
> Serve Jahve with fear,
> And rejoice with trembling.
> Kiss the Son, lest He be angry and ye perish,
> For His wrath may kindle suddenly —
> Blessed are all they who hide in Him!
> (Psalm 2:10-12 Keil and Delitzsch)

All are urged to submit to him and pledge their loyalty. Rebellion is futile and only draws judgment, whereas submission and loyalty are followed by blessing. The coming Messiah is pictured here as a divine King and is to be recognized as such by all the world.

Psalm 45 also refers to the coming King. Here the psalmist declares:

> My heart overflows with goodly speech,
> I say to myself: "My production is concerning a king,"
> My tongue is the pen of a quick writer.
> With beauty art thou arrayed beyond the children of men,
> Gracefulness is shed upon thy lips;
> Therefore hath Elohim blessed thee for ever.
> (Psalm 45:1,2 Keil and Delitzsch)

The psalmist states that he is speaking of a good matter, that which pictures the coming King. He glorifies this King and places him above all men in beauty and glory. Not only does the coming King exceed men in beauty and glory, but divine grace fills his mouth as he speaks of the wondrous things of God. As the divinely appointed King, he is blessed before God forever.

The psalmist expands the glory and majesty of the coming King in another Psalm when he says:

> You have gone up on high; You have led captivity captive;
> You have received gifts for men. Yes, for the rebellious
> also, that the LORD God might dwell among them.
> (Psalm 68:18 KJ II)

With these words the psalmist points to the work of atonement which the King will successfully carry out. Having carried out the work of atonement, he will ascend into heaven and reign. The result of his ascension and reign will be that man's captivity under sin and Satan is carried away captive. Man's captivity under sin is nullified. Great blessings are available for all men, even for those who are rebellious and do not believe. Through the atonement God is reconciled to mankind and will dwell with them here in time with his invisible presence and hereafter with his visible presence to all eternity.

In Psalm 110 David says of the coming King:

> The oracle of Jahve unto my Lord:
> "Sit thou at My right hand,
> Until I make thine enemies
> The stool of thy feet."
> The sceptre of thy might
> Will Jahve stretch forth out of Zion:
> "Rule thou in the midst of thine enemies!"
> Thy people are most willing on thy field-day;
> In holy festive garments,
> Out of the womb of the morning's dawn
> Cometh the dew of thy young men.
> Jahve hath sworn and will not repent:
> "Thou shalt be a priest for ever
> After the manner of Melchizedek."
> The Lord at thy right hand
> Dasheth kings in pieces in the day of His wrath,
> He shall judge among the nations,
> It becometh full of corpses.
> He dasheth in pieces a head upon a broad country;
> Of the brook in the way shall he drink,
> Therefore shall he lift up the head on high.
> (Psalm 110:1-7 Keil and Delitzsch)

In these words David, great king that he was, called the coming King his Lord and pointed to his universal reign. His reign would not be just one of power, but it would be one established in sacrifice and atonement. The coming King would bear the priesthood just as Melchizedek did, not being preceded or succeeded by a priest of lineal descent. In his hand would be placed the judgment of all men. He would be filled with the water of life and by virtue of this would be the one to whom all would look for life and salvation. He would be Melchizedek in the fullest sense, the King of Righteousness — the one in whom all could live, the one by whom many would die because of their unbelief.

Just as David, the "Sweet Singer" of Israel, sang of the coming Messiah, so also David's son, Solomon, sang of him and said:

> Give the king Your judgments, O God, and Your right-
> eousness to the king's son. He shall judge Your people
> with righteousness and Your poor with judgment. The
> mountains shall bring peace to the people, and the little
> hills, with righteousness. He shall judge the poor of the
> people; He shall save the children of the needy and shall
> crush the cruel one. They shall fear You as long as the sun
> and moon endure, throughout all generations. He shall
> come down like rain on the mown grass, like showers that
> water the earth. In His days the righteous shall flourish;
> and abundance of peace as long as the moon endures. He
> shall also have the rule from sea to sea, and from the river
> to the ends of the earth. Those who dwell in the wilderness
> shall bow before Him; and His enemies shall lick the dust.
> The kings of Tarshish and of the isles shall bring presents;
> the kings of Sheba and Seba shall offer gifts. Yes, all kings
> shall fall down before Him; all nations shall serve Him.
> For He shall deliver the needy when he cries; the poor
> also, and him who has no helper. He shall have pity on the
> poor and needy; and He saves the souls of the needy. He

shall redeem their soul from deceit and violence; and their blood shall be precious in His sight. And he shall live, and to him shall be given the gold of Sheba, for He shall pray for him continually. He shall be blessed all day long. There shall be a handful of grain in the earth on the top of the mountains; the fruit of it shall shake like Lebanon; and they of the city shall flourish like grass of the earth. His name shall endure forever; His name shall be continued as long as the sun; and men shall be blessed in Him; all nations shall call Him blessed. Blessed is the LORD God, the God of Israel, who alone does wonderful things. And blessed is His glorious name forever; and the whole earth is filled with His glory! Amen and amen. (Psalm 72:1-19 KJ II)

Solomon had become king, but as he penned these words, he saw a King far greater than he or his father had been, far greater than any earthly king. He saw a kingdom far greater than any earthly kingdom. He saw a King filled with divine righteousness and holiness, wielding divine judgment, One before whom all kings and all nations will bow. The kingdom of this King would endure to the end of time and into eternity. The glory of his kingdom would never fade but would rather increase. Solomon here saw the Messiah as King. He, Solomon, was but a type, a symbol of the mighty King to come.

Isaiah

The coming of the Priest-King was an event which would have tremendous impact for the world. It would validate all the past promises of God. It would show the truth of his mission of salvation and would underscore the certain fulfillment of God's promises for the future. The prophet Isaiah was blessed perhaps more than any other man with the vision of what the day of God's Messiah King would be like and what it would bring to the world. Isaiah writes:

> Nevertheless, there will be no more gloom for those who were in distress. In the past he humbled the land of Zebulun and the land of Naphtali, but in the future he will honor Galilee of the Gentiles, by the way of the sea, along the Jordan — The people walking in darkness have seen a great light; on those living in the land of the shadow of death a light has dawned. You have enlarged the nation and increased their joy; they rejoice before you as people rejoice at the harvest, as men rejoice when dividing the plunder. For as in the day of Midian's defeat, you have shattered the yoke that burdens them, the bar across their shoulders, the rod of their oppressor. Every warrior's boot used in battle and every garment rolled in blood will be destined for burning, will be fuel for the fire. For to us a child is born, to us a son is given, and the government will be on his shoulders. And he will be called Wonderful Counselor, Mighty God, Everlasting Father, Prince of Peace. Of the increase of his government and peace there will be no end. He will reign on David's throne and over his kingdom, establishing and upholding it with justice and righteousness from that time on and forever. The zeal of the LORD Almighty will accomplish this. (Isaiah 9:1-7 NIV)

Looking down over the vast expanse of seven centuries, Isaiah foresaw the birth of the Messiah King. He would be born as a human son but in reality would be a divine Son, the Son of God. In him the reign of heaven and earth would be centered. Isaiah used many names to describe him. He would be the Mighty God. He would be the everlasting Father, the One who participated in the creation of all living beings. He would be the Prince, the One in whom all would be given peace from God.

His rule and kingdom would last forever. He would come from the earthly royal line of David, but he would be eternally established in his kingship in divine judgment and justice.

His presence would be seen and felt. He would shine as a light upon the land of God's people, especially in the area of Galilee. The people who were walking in spiritual darkness would see in him the light of salvation. He would bring joy and deliverance to his people, but his coming would also bring about God's judgment on his foes.

Time after time Isaiah beholds the coming of the King with awe and wonder. In one marvelous vision Isaiah sees him as a mighty warrior who is the only hope for mankind:

> And He saw that there was no man, and He wondered that there was no intercessor. Therefore His own arm brought salvation to Him; and His righteousness sustained Him. For He put on righteousness like a breastplate, and a helmet of salvation on His head. And He put on the garments of vengeance for clothing and was covered with zeal for a robe. According to works, that way He will repay: fury to His foes, deed for deed to His enemies; He repays their deeds to the isles. So they shall fear the name of the LORD from the west, and His glory from the east — when the enemy comes in like a flood, the LORD's Spirit shall raise a banner against him. And the Redeemer shall come to Zion, and to those who turn from transgression in Jacob, says the LORD. (Isaiah 59:16-20 KJ II)

The battle of redemption, the destruction of the power of sin and death and hell would be Christ's alone. No man would be able to participate in the fight, for all mankind needed to be redeemed. The Messiah King, because of man's helplessness, would win the battle of salvation with his own mighty arm. His holiness and righteousness would be invincible. He would wear it as a breastplate and the salvation of men would be his helmet. Vengeance and judgment would be his clothing and his cloak would be divine zeal. He would be the victor in the battle against his foes and would deal with them in just anger. From one end of the earth to the other his name would be feared and honored. He would be the protection of God's people from all their foes.

Toward the end of his book Isaiah again pictures the mighty Messiah King as a warrior. This time he is seen returning from battle against his foes. In majestic strides he marches forward in triumph. His garments are blood-stained and his appearance awesome.

As Isaiah sees him approaching, he calls out:

> Who is this coming from Edom, from Bozrah, with his garments stained crimson? Who is this, robed in splendor, striding forward in the greatness of his strength?

The great Warrior King replies in awesome fashion:

> "It is I, speaking in righteousness, mighty to save."

Again the prophet calls out and asks:

> Why are your garments red, like those of one treading the winepress?

The mighty Victor answers in an even more awesome manner:

> "I have trodden the winepress alone; from the nations no one was with me. I trampled them in my anger and trod them down in my wrath; their blood spattered my garments, and I stained all my clothing. For the day of vengeance was in my heart, and the year of my redemption has come. I looked, but there was no one to help, I was appalled that no one gave support; so my own arm worked salvation for me, and my own wrath sustained me. I trampled the nations in my anger; in my wrath I made them drunk and poured their blood on the ground."
> (Isaiah 63:1-6 NIV)

This passage sets before us a picture of the triumphant Messiah King. He comes to his people in triumph from the land of their foes, here pictured as Edom. In his blood-stained clothing he bears the marks of a furious battle. When asked about himself and his garments, he replies that he has had to fight the battle alone. In his lonely fight, his great strength and fury upheld him and he totally destroyed his foes. And in his victory the time of redemption has arrived for his people.

Other Prophets

The prophet Micah, who lived at the same time Isaiah did, added to the certainty and clarity of the picture of the Messiah. Micah names Bethlehem as the town of Christ's birth:

> And you, Bethlehem Ephratah, you who are little among the thousands of Judah, out of you He shall come forth to

Me to be ruler of Israel, He whose goings forth have been from of old, from everlasting. (Micah 5:2 KJ II)

What a comforting and beautiful hope these prophecies set before God's people! In the days of Isaiah and Micah things looked very gloomy for the people of God. Israel and Syria had joined together to destroy Judah. There did not seem to be anyone who could or would help them. How these words must have strengthened their faith and hope and centered their thoughts in the coming Messiah!

Years later things looked even worse. God's people were in captivity in Babylon. It seemed that they had been forsaken. A return from the captivity seemed impossible. In this dark hour the prophet Ezekiel was sent to them. In his prophecy he bids them look to the coming Messiah King. This time the coming King is not portrayed in might, power, majesty and triumph, but in love, tenderness, wisdom and protection:

> And I will raise up over them one shepherd. And He shall feed them: My servant David, He shall feed them; and He shall be to them for a shepherd. And I Jehovah will be their God; and My servant David a ruler among them; I Jehovah have spoken. (Ezekiel 34:23,24 Gr.)

Shorn of all earthly might and dominion, God's people would retain their greatest blessing and hope. They would remain God's flock. Though earthly armies would not be theirs, they would have One arise from their midst who would be infinitely greater than any army or combination of armies. The Messiah King would be their Prince. He would come to gather, protect, save and guide his people as only a true and divine Shepherd could. Descended from David's royal line, he would be the second David, the Messiah King, their Shepherd King.

In words of comfort the prophet Ezekiel urges God's people to look beyond the period of captivity and slavery to a better day, a more glorious time, saying:

> And David My servant shall be king over them. And they shall all have one Shepherd. They shall also walk in My judgments and obey My laws, and do them. And they shall dwell in the land that I have given to Jacob My servant, the land in which your fathers have lived. And they shall live in it, they and their children, and their children's children forever. And My servant David shall be their king forever. And I will make a covenant of peace with them. It shall be an everlasting covenant with them. And I will place them and multiply them, and I will set My sanctuary in their midst forevermore. Also My tabernacle shall be with them. Yes, I will be their God, and they shall be My people. (Ezekiel 37:24-27 KJ II)

Again Ezekiel points them to the time of the coming of the Messiah King, the Shepherd King, the second David. His coming would usher in the Messianic age in which the glory and salvation of God would be carried to the ends of the earth. People from every land would know that God had established his everlasting covenant with his people, that he would make his dwelling among them and would sanctify them to be his own.

While the prophet Ezekiel proclaimed the tidings of the coming Messiah to God's people in the places where they lived during the exile, the prophet Daniel labored in the palace. He testified to the ruler of Babylon about the coming Messiah. During Daniel's early years at court,

Nebuchadnezzar the king had a dream concerning the coming kingdoms of the world and demanded an interpretation. God enabled Daniel to interpret it. He stated that in the days of the third world empire after Babylon, God would establish an eternal kingdom through One whom he would send. In this way God not only unfolded future history to Nebuchadnezzar, but also set before him the person and time of the coming Messiah. Daniel's words are still amazing today. He said:

> You watched until a stone was cut out without hands, which struck the image on its feet of iron and clay and broke them to pieces. Then the iron, the clay, the bronze, the silver and the gold were broken to pieces together; becoming like the chaff of the summer threshing floors. And the wind carried them away, so that no place was found for them. And the stone that struck the image became a great mountain and filled the whole earth.
>
> And in the days of these kings, the God of Heaven shall set up a kingdom which shall never be destroyed. And the kingdom shall not be left to other people. It shall break in pieces and destroy all these kingdoms, and it shall stand forever. Because you saw that the stone was cut out of the mountain without hands, and that it broke in pieces the iron, the bronze, the silver and the gold — the great God has made known to the king what shall happen in the future. And the dream is certain, and the meaning of it is sure. (Daniel 2:34,35,44,45 KJ II)

Years later, Daniel was granted some other tremendous visions by God. Daniel describes one of them in the following manner:

> I saw in the night visions, and, behold, one like the Son of man came with the clouds of heaven, and He came to the Ancient of Days. And they brought Him near before

> Him. And there was given to Him dominion and glory, and a kingdom, that all people, nations and languages should serve Him. His dominion is an everlasting dominion which shall not pass away, and His kingdom is that which shall not be destroyed. (Daniel 7:13,14 KJ II)

In the vision Daniel looked into heaven and saw the triumphant Savior brought before the throne of heaven. Into his hands was placed all power, dominion and judgment. Through him all the enemies of God's people were destroyed. In him an everlasting kingdom was established. This Ruler of heaven would be the Messiah, the Christ who would rule all things for the welfare of his people and would someday lead them to glory.

After the Babylonian Captivity God again sent prophets to his people. One of these was the prophet Zechariah. He said of the coming Messiah:

> And speak to him saying, Thus speaks the LORD of hosts, saying, Behold! the Man whose name is THE BRANCH! And He shall grow up out of His place and He shall build the temple of the LORD. Even He shall build the temple of the LORD. And He shall bear the glory and shall sit and rule on His throne. And He shall be a priest on His throne. And the counsel of peace shall be between them both. (Zechariah 6:12,13 KJ II)

Here Zechariah names the coming Great One, "The Branch." He says the Branch will build the "temple" of God, in other words, reestablish the worship of the true God among God's people. Not only would he establish God's kingdom among them, but he would be the King within it.

Moreover, centuries before Jesus entered Jerusalem on

Palm Sunday, Zechariah saw the day when this King would come to Jerusalem in humility, riding on a donkey:

> Rejoice greatly, O daughter of Zion! Shout, daughter of Jerusalem! See, your king comes to you, righteous and having salvation, gentle and riding on a donkey, on a colt, the foal of a donkey. (Zechariah 9:9 NIV)

In that day, the people were not to be deceived by the lowly way in which he would come. For, in spite of his humility, he would be the bearer of salvation to all mankind.

Malachi, the last prophet of the Old Testament, brings the prophecies of the coming Messiah to a close when he says:

> But to you who fear My name, the Sun of righteousness shall arise with healing in His wings. And you shall go forth and grow up like calves of the stall. (Malachi 4:2 KJ II)

The Messiah is pictured here as the divine Sun of Righteousness who would come to help and heal his people. In him they would find security, peace, prosperity and blessing.

The concept of the coming Messiah as King was commonly held by people at Jesus' time. This can readily be seen in the words of the Wise Men who came to worship Christ as their heaven-sent King. They asked publicly in Jerusalem:

> Where is He who has been born king of the Jews? For we have seen His star in the east and have come to worship Him. (Matthew 2:2 KJ II)

Not only was their question understood, but it was

answered by the scribes in the naming of Bethlehem as the birthplace of the King, according to the prophecy of Micah.

4. THE ANGEL OF THE LORD
— THE MAL'AKH JAHWEH

Angels

As one studies the Bible, it soon becomes evident that God created beings called angels, in addition to man. When the Bible uses the term angel (in Hebrew, mal'akh), it is referring to living, invisible, celestial or heavenly beings created by God along with all other creatures at some time during the six days of creation. God declares this in Exodus:

> For in six days Jehovah made the heavens and the earth, the sea, and all which is in them, and He rested on the seventh day; therefore Jehovah blessed the Sabbath day and sanctified it. (Exodus 20:11 Gr.)

These beings are holy, wise and extremely powerful:

> [Jesus said:] "For whoever is ashamed of Me and My teachings, of him the Son of Man will be ashamed when He comes in His own glory and His Father's and of the holy angels." (Luke 9:26 Ber.)

> Bless the Lord, you His angels who abound with strength, who carry out His orders, listening to the sound of His Word! (Psalm 103:20 Ber.)

> This will happen when the Lord Jesus is revealed from heaven in blazing fire with his powerful angels. (2 Thessalonians 1:7 NIV)

Scripture calls them messengers — the Old Testament Hebrew term for angel as well as the New Testament

Greek both mean "messenger." Angels, then, serve as God's messengers. Sent from God, they care for and protect all Christians throughout the world:

> Are not all angels ministering spirits sent to serve those who will inherit salvation? (Hebrews 1:14 NIV)
>
> For He shall give His angels charge over you, to keep you in all your ways. They shall bear you up in their hands lest you dash your foot on a stone. (Psalm 91:11,12 Gr.)
>
> Take care that you do not despise one of these little ones, for I say to you that their angels in Heaven continually look upon the face of My Father who is in Heaven. (Matthew 18:10 KJ II)

The holy angels have as their one aim the glorification of God. At no time in the entire Bible did they ever permit a man to offer to them any sacrifice, worship or glory. The Bible is very explicit in stating that all such honor belongs to God and God alone:

> Then Jesus said to him, Get away, Satan! For it is written, "You shall worship the LORD your God, and Him alone you shall serve." (Matthew 4:10 KJ II)
>
> Do not worship any other god, for the LORD, whose name is Jealous, is a jealous God. (Exodus 34:14 NIV)

It should be noted that this is what the angel told St. John when he fell down to worship him:

> But he said to me, "Do not do it! I am a fellow servant with you and with your brothers the prophets and of all who keep the words of this book. Worship God!" (Revelation 22:9 NIV)

J.T. Mueller in his *Christian Dogmatics* says that the existence of angels cannot be proved by reason, but must be drawn from Scripture which teaches their existence from Genesis to Revelation in such passages as:

> He drove out the man and placed cherubim east of the
> Eden garden with a flaming sword turning in every direc-
> tion to guard the path to the tree of life. (Genesis 3:24
> Ber.)

> And Jacob went on his way, and the angels of God met
> him. And when Jacob saw them he said, This is the camp
> of God; and he called the name of that place, Mahanaim.
> (Genesis 32:1,2 Gr.)

> He makes His angels spirits, His ministers a flaming fire.
> (Psalm 104:4 KJ II)

> In the year that King Uzziah died, then I saw the Lord
> sitting on a throne, high and lifted up — and His train
> filled the temple. Above it stood the seraphim. Each one
> had six wings; with two he covered his face, and with two
> he covered his feet, and with two he flew. And one cried to
> another and said, Holy, holy, holy, is Jehovah of hosts;
> the whole earth is full of His glory! And the doorposts
> shook from the voice of the one who cried; and the house
> was filled with smoke. Then I said, Woe to me! For I am
> undone; for I am a man of unclean lips, and I live amongst
> a people of unclean lips; for my eyes have seen the King,
> Jehovah of hosts. Then one of the seraphim flew to me
> with a live coal in his hand, snatched with tongs from the
> altar. And he touched it on my mouth and said, See, this
> has touched your lips; and your iniquity is taken away,
> and your sin is covered. (Isaiah 6:1-7 Gr.)

> Then war developed in heaven, Michael and his angels
> battling against the dragon, and the dragon with his an-
> gels waging war. (Revelation 12:7 Ber.)

Mueller goes on to say that the term "angel," by which
the Bible designates this class of created, finite and invisible beings, does not describe their essence but their office
and signifies "one sent," or a "messenger." The nature of

the angels is described by the term "spirit." An angel is then a spiritual being, having a mind and will but no body.

That the name "angel" is a designation of office is clear from the fact that Scripture ascribes it:

a) to ministers of the divine Word in the Bible:

> For the priest's lips should keep knowledge and they should seek the law at his mouth for he is the messenger [mal'akh] of the LORD of hosts. (Malachi 2:7 KJ II)

> This is the one of whom it is written: *I will send My messenger ahead of You to prepare Your way before You.* (Matthew 11:10 AAT)

b) to the Son of God, the "uncreated Angel," as the supreme and unique Messenger of God of the Old Testament:

> Behold, I am sending My messenger, and he shall prepare the way before Me, And the Lord, whom you seek, shall suddenly come to His temple, even the Angel of the Covenant, in whom you delight. Behold, He comes, says Jehovah of hosts. (Malachi 3:1 Gr.)

> "God so loved the world that He gave His only Son so that everyone who believes in Him doesn't perish but has everlasting life. You see, God didn't send His Son into the world to condemn the world but to save the world through Him. The One whom God has sent says what God says because God gives Him His Spirit without a limit." (John 3:16,17,34 AAT)

> In all their affliction, He was not a foe; and the Angel of His face saved them; in His love and in His pity He redeemed them. And he bore them and carried them all the days of old. (Isaiah 63:9 Gr.)

> Then Jacob blessed Joseph: "God, before whom my fathers Abraham and Isaac walked, God, who has been my Shepherd all my life till now, the angel who delivered me

from all evil, bless the young men. Let them be called by my name and the name of my fathers Abraham and Isaac." (Genesis 48:15,16 AAT)

The Angel of the Lord

Some things need to be noted as we begin to study the Mal'akh. Although the Hebrew language has a definite article or "the," it does not always use it as we do in English. Even when the noun is definite it is not always used. As a result, in some translations "the" is sometimes added for emphasis and clarity or omitted according to the belief and understanding of the translator. Unfortunately, *the* Mal'akh is not recognized as definitely and fully as he should be by all; as a result he is often merely referred to as "an angel." This makes him a created angel rather than "the Angel" and deprives him of the glory and honor of being the divine Messenger of God or Jesus in the Old Testament. Translations which do not recognize his divine stature and role are in error.

The Hebrew word mal'akh is a word which can denote a visible human messenger of God, an invisible angelic messenger of God or the uncreated, divine Messenger of God — Christ Jesus, the Second Person of the Trinity, true God himself. To distinguish between men and angels is not very difficult or confusing; but to distinguish between created angels and the uncreated Messenger of God has caused much confusion through the centuries. The true identity and role of the divine Mal'akh has often been obscured or denied.

Yet if one carefully examines the appearances and references to angels in the Bible, a striking difference will often become apparent. Angels guarded the tree of life. Groups of angels were seen by Jacob and Gehazi. God sent Michael, the Archangel, to drive Satan from Moses' body. Angels were seen in visions by the prophets. An angel appeared to Zechariah and to Mary. A group of angels appeared to the shepherds. Angels appeared to Philip, Peter and Paul. John saw and spoke with angels. Individual angels guard God's children. It can readily be seen that all these activities are similar and are duties we would expect of a creature which was created to serve God and man. The actions are limited to announcements, opening locked shackles and doors, transporting believers, rebuking Satan and guarding what God has assigned them to guard.

In addition to these references to God's angels, which all will admit involve created spiritual beings, there are a large number of appearances and references to a Mal'akh or Angel whose actions can often be called elemental, they are so tremendous. His actions and appearances are always associated with the formation, the protection, the judging, the delivering of God's people. His role is consistently Messianic and consistently a role that shapes history, judges nations and wields almighty powers. Whatever the Mal'akh does seems to affect a people, a nation or the world. These references quite evidently do not refer to created beings but to the uncreated Messenger of God, Christ Jesus, carrying out his Savior role in the Old Testament.

One other facet should be considered. God is a God of order. He is consistent. What he says he will do, he does.

Scripture very plainly states that the Mal'akh said that he would make Abraham into a great nation. In keeping with this, the Mal'akh guided Israel out of Egypt and on to the Promised Land. He helped them conquer it. He shielded them from Balaam's curse. He rebuked them publicly for their godlessness. He sent judges or deliverers to free them. But why stop his appearances here and say that only created angels appear hereafter? Scripture shows that the Mal'akh appeared in the time of the kings and again during the exile to help God's people. The last of the prophets, Malachi (whose name, incidentally, means "my messenger"), refers to the Mal'akh as being a delight to God's people. He must then have been well known, revered and loved. His task was to shape God's people and prepare the world for his birth as the Savior. It is tragic if we do not let his Messianic Old Testament role shine in all its beauty.

The Old Testament presents a wide variety of pictures of this special, divine Mal'akh, for he appears often. He is recognized as God; he is called God by Scripture; he calls himself God. He accepts sacrifices, is worshiped, forgives sin, carries out God's judgments, is obeyed by angels, rebukes Satan, is obeyed by, loved by, and known to the Old Testament saints simply as "the Mal'akh," "the Mal'akh Jahweh" (Angel of the Lord), or "the Mal'akh Elohim" (Angel of God). His acts affect nations and even the world. The writers of the Old Testament use his title interchangeably with that of God himself. As we shall see, Stephen in the New Testament identifies him as God, while Paul identifies him as God and Christ.

In this study, we will consider four facets of the Mal-'akh: 1) his divine role in history; 2) his divine power of judgment; 3) his divine person and mission; 4) the recognition of him and his divinity in the New Testament.

The Mal'akh's Power over History and Nations

Early Appearances of the Mal'akh

History has had many crises dictated or shaped by varying influences, which in turn resulted in a myriad number of solutions. No single being, however, has appeared at more critical times or effected more determining influences than the Mal'akh Jahweh in the history of the Old Testament Hebrew people.

Scripture first refers to the Mal'akh in the days of Abraham:

> And the Angel of Jehovah found her by a fountain of water in the wilderness; by the fountain in the way of Shur. And He said, Hagar, Sarai's maid, where did you come from? And where do you go? And she said, I am fleeing from the face of my mistress, Sarai. And the Angel of Jehovah said to her, Return to your mistress and submit yourself under her hands. And the Angel of Jehovah said to her, I will exceedingly multiply your seed, so that it shall not be numbered for multitude. And the Angel of Jehovah said to her, See, you are with child and shall bear a son; and you shall call his name Ishmael, because Jehovah has attended to your affliction. And he shall be a wild ass of a man; his hand against everyone; and the hand of everyone against him; and he shall live before all his brothers. And she called the name of Jehovah, the One speaking to her, You, a God of vision! For she said, Even here have I looked after the One seeing me? Therefore the well was called, The Well of the Living One Seeing Me. Behold, it is between Kadesh and Bered. (Genesis 16:7-14 Gr.)

Here we find that the Mal'akh halted the flight of Hagar from Sarai, Abram's wife. He instructed her to return to Sarai with the promise that he would build a powerful nation from her son, Ishmael. He claims for himself the power of shaping this part of history and of developing this nation.

Years later Hagar and Ishmael were compelled to leave the home of Abraham because of Isaac, the promised son of Abraham and Sarah. Scripture describes what happened in these words:

> And Abraham rose early in the morning, and took bread and a skin of water, and gave them to Hagar, putting them on her shoulder, and the child, and sent her away. And she left and wandered in the wilderness of Beer-sheba. And the water was consumed from the skin and she put the child under one of the shrubs. And she went and sat down about a bowshot away, across from him. For she said, let me not see the death of the child; and she sat across from him and raised her voice and wept. And God heard the voice of the young boy; and the angel of God called to Hagar out of the heavens, and he said to her, what is wrong with you, Hagar? Do not fear, for God has heard the voice of the boy, where he is. Get up, lift up the boy and hold him up with your hand; for I will make a great nation of him. And God opened her eyes, and she saw a well of water; and she went and filled the skin with water, and gave drink to the young boy.
>
> And God was with the boy, and he grew up, and he lived in the wilderness, and became an archer. And he lived in the wilderness of Paran; and his mother took a wife for him out of the land of Egypt. (Genesis 21:14-21 Gr.)

Here we are told that when Hagar and Ishmael had used up all their water, Hagar placed Ishmael under a desert tree to die and went a short distance away so that she would not have to witness his death. Ishmael pleaded for help and God answered his plea. We are told the Mal'akh of God or Elohim comforted Hagar, promised life to the boy and said he would make a great nation of him. We are told that Elohim then showed her a spring and that he was with Ishmael and blessed him. The divine name, Elohim, is used interchangeably with the Mal'akh, thus pointing to the divinity of the Mal'akh.

Later God tested Abraham's faith by ordering him to sacrifice Isaac as a burnt offering. Scripture says of this appearance of the Mal'akh:

> And they came to the place which God had named to him, and Abraham built an altar there and arranged the wood; and he bound his son Isaac and laid him on the altar on the wood. And Abraham stretched out his hand and took the knife to slay his son. And the Angel of Jehovah called to him from the heavens, and said, Abraham! Abraham! And he said, I am here. And He said, Do not lay your hand on the boy, nor do anything to him. For now I know that you are a God-fearer, and you have not withheld your son, your only one, from Me. And Abraham lifted up his eyes and looked; and behold! A ram behind him was entangled in a thicket by its horns. And Abraham went and took the ram and offered him for a burnt offering instead of his son. And Abraham called the name of that place Jehovah-jireh; so that it is said until this day, In the mount Jehovah will provide.
>
> And the Angel of Jehovah called to Abraham out of Heaven the second time. And said, I have sworn by Myself, says Jehovah, because you have done this thing, and have not withheld your son, your only son, that in blessing I will bless you, and in multiplying I will multiply your

seed like the stars of the sky, and like the sand which is on the seashore. And your Seed shall possess the gate of His enemies. And in your Seed shall all the nations of the earth be blessed, because you have obeyed My voice. (Genesis 22:9-18 Gr.)

When Abraham did not refuse to obey God even to the point of sacrificing Isaac, the Mal'akh promised that he would make of his descendants a great nation. Furthermore, from this nation a Seed would arise in whom all the families of the earth would be blessed. The shaping of this history was within the Mal'akh's power.

Years later when Jacob had to flee to his uncle Laban because he had stolen his brother Esau's blessing, the Mal'akh appeared to him in a dream at Bethel. We read:

And he dreamed; and, behold, a ladder was placed on the earth, its top reaching to the heavens; and, behold, the angels of God ascending and descending on it! And, behold, Jehovah stood above it and said, I am Jehovah, the God of your father Abraham, and the God of Isaac; the land on which you are lying I will give to you and to your seed. And your seed shall be like the dust of the earth, and you shall spread to the west and to the east and to the north and to the south; and the families of all the earth shall be blessed in you and in your seed. And, behold, I will be with you, and will guard you in every place in which you may go, and will bring you back to this land; for I will not forsake you until I have surely done that which I have spoken to you. And Jacob awakened from his sleep and said, Surely Jehovah is in this place, and I did not know. And he was afraid, and said, How fearful is this place! This is nothing except the house of God, and this is the gateway to Heaven. And Jacob rose early in the morning, and took the stone which he had put at his head, and placed it as a memorial; and he poured oil on the top of it. And he called the name of that place, The House of God — and yet, Luz was the name of the city at first. And Jacob vowed a vow saying, If God is with me and keeps me in this way which I am traveling, and gives to me bread to eat and clothing to wear, and I return in peace to the house of my father, then Jehovah shall become my God, and this stone which I have placed as a memorial pillar shall become the house of God; and all which You shall give to me, I will tithe the tenth to You. (Genesis 28:12-22 Gr.)

Scripture sheds a great deal of light on this passage. A number of years after Jacob's dream of the ladder, Jacob described to his wives an appearance of the Mal'akh to him:

And the Angel of God spoke to me in a dream, Jacob! And I said, I am here. And he said, Lift up your eyes and see all the rams that are leaping on the flock; they are striped, speckled, and mottled. For I have seen all that Laban is doing to you. I am the God of Bethel, where you anointed the pillar, where you vowed a vow to Me. Now rise up, go out of this land and return to the land of your kindred. (Genesis 31:11-13 Gr.)

Here we note that the Mal'akh called himself "the God of Bethel." He, then, is the One who promised to give the land of Canaan to Jacob and his descendants. Thus the future ownership of the land of Canaan was determined by the decree of the Mal'akh.

Appearances to Moses and the Israelites

The subsequent history of Jacob and his family is well known to all of us. It includes the sale of Joseph into slavery in Egypt where the family of Israel grew into the nation of Israel.

In the book of Exodus the Mal'akh again appeared, this time to Moses in the burning bush:

> And the Angel of Jehovah appeared to him in a flame of fire from the middle of a thorn bush; and he looked, and behold, the thorn bush was burning with fire, and the thorn bush was not burned up! And Moses said, I will turn aside now and see this great sight, why the thorn bush is not burned up. And Jehovah saw that he turned aside to see, and God called to him from the midst of the thorn bush, and said, Moses! Moses! And he said, I am here. And He said, Do not come near here, pull off your sandals from your feet, for the place on which you are standing is holy ground. And He said, I am the God of your fathers, the God of Abraham, the God of Isaac, and the God of Jacob; and Moses hid his face, for he feared to look upon God. (Exodus 3:2-6 Gr.)

The Mal'akh then commanded Moses to go to Egypt and lead Israel out of slavery. Moses was told that the Mal'akh would bring the Israelites safely out of Egypt, lead them to Canaan, and dispossess the inhabitants so that they would have the Promised Land. In the power of the Mal'akh, Moses went to Egypt and after the ten plagues led his people out as the Mal'akh had promised. As they left Egypt Scripture says:

> And Jehovah was going before them by day in a pillar of cloud, to lead them in the way; and by night in a pillar of fire, to give light to them, to go by day and by night. The pillar of cloud did not cease by day, and the pillar of fire by night, before the people. (Exodus 13:21,22 Gr.)

> And the Angel of God withdrew, the One going before the

camp of Israel, and He went behind them, and the pillar of cloud withdrew from before them, and it stood behind them. (Exodus 14:19 Gr.)

It is interesting to note that in the Exodus 13 passage we are told that Jehovah was in the cloudy pillar. In Exodus 14 we are told that the Mal'akh was in the pillar of cloud. Here the name of Jahweh is used interchangeably with that of the Mal'akh, thus showing his divinity. He led his people through the Red Sea and through the wilderness to Mt. Sinai. For the next forty years the visible presence of the Mal'akh was with Israel by day in a pillar of cloud and by night in a pillar of fire.

Later as Israel prepares to leave Mt. Sinai for the Promised Land, God says:

Behold, I am about to send an Angel before you, to guard you in the way, and to bring you to the place which I have prepared. Be careful before Him, and listen to His voice; do not be rebellious against Him; for He will not forgive your transgressions, for My name is in Him. (Exodus 23:20,21 Gr.)

In this passage Jahweh addressed his people directly, saying that he would send his Mal'akh ahead of them to lead them into the land of Canaan. God warned the Israelites not to provoke the Mal'akh or disobey him, for he, the Mal'akh, would not pardon their transgressions. This power was attributed to him because the name of God was within him. Jahweh himself attested to the divine power residing within the Mal'akh, even declaring that the power of judgment for sin belonged to the Mal-'akh.

Moses in a letter to Edom speaks of the constant guidance of the Mal'akh who brought them out of Egypt. He says:

> But when we cried out to the LORD, He heard our plea and sent an angel to bring us out of Egypt. Now here we are at Kadesh, a town near the border of your territory. (Numbers 20:16 Ber.)

As the conquest of the land of Canaan by Israel became evident to the heathen, they reacted in terror. In the book of Numbers we come to the story of Balaam, a soothsayer, who was hired by King Balak of Moab to curse Israel. Scripture says of Balaam:

> And God's anger was kindled because he went. And the Angel of Jehovah stationed Himself in the way, as an enemy against him; and he was riding on his ass, and two of his servants were with him. And the ass saw the Angel of Jehovah standing in the way, and His sword drawn in His hand; and the ass turned out of the way and went into a field; and Balaam smote the ass to turn it back into the way. And the Angel of Jehovah stood in a narrow path of the vineyards, a wall being on this side and a wall on that. And the ass saw the Angel of Jehovah and she thrust herself to the wall and crushed Balaam's foot against the wall; and he smote her again. And the Angel of Jehovah went further and stood in a narrow place, where there was no way to turn, either to the right hand or to the left. And the ass saw the Angel of Jehovah, and she lay down under Balaam; and Balaam's anger was kindled, and he smote the ass with his staff. And Jehovah opened the mouth of the ass, and she said to Balaam, What have I done to you, that you have beaten me these three times? And Balaam said to the ass, Because you have done too much to me; oh that there were a sword in my hand, for now I would kill

you. And the ass said to Balaam, Am I not your ass, on which you have ridden all your life long to this day? Was I ever known to do so to you? And he said, No. Then Jehovah opened the eyes of Balaam, and he saw the Angel of Jehovah standing in the way, with His sword drawn in His hand; and he bowed his head and fell on his face. And the Angel of Jehovah said to him, Why have you struck your ass these three times? Behold, I have come out as an enemy because your way is contrary to Me. And the ass saw Me, and turned aside before Me these three times; if she had not turned aside from Me, surely now I would have killed you, and saved her alive. And Balaam said to the Angel of Jehovah, I have sinned ; for I did not know that You stood in the way against me; now, if evil is in Your eyes, I shall turn back myself. And the Angel of Jehovah said to Balaam, Go with the men; and only the word which I speak to you, you shall speak it; and Balaam went with the chiefs of Balak. . . . And Balaam said to Balak, See, I have come to you; now, am I able to speak anything at all? The word which God puts in my mouth, that I will speak. (Numbers 22:22-35,38 Gr.)

Balaam had been told by God not to go to curse the Israelites. But being tempted by money and hoping God would relent, he went with the enemies of the Jews anyway. We are told that Elohim — the High, the Mighty God — was angry with Balaam for going. Upon seeing the Mal'akh, Balaam's ass shied off the path, then when it again saw the Mal'akh before it, it jammed Balaam's foot against a wall. When it saw the Mal'akh the third time it fell down and rebuked Balaam when he punished it for refusing to proceed in the presence of the Mal'akh. Balaam was then granted the vision of the ass and saw the Mal'akh Jahweh standing before him. He was told by the

Mal'akh that his behavior was sinful and worthy of death, whereupon Balaam begged for forgiveness. He was told to speak only what the Mal'akh told him. Balaam acknowledged the divinity of the Mal'akh when he later stated that he could only utter what God told him.

In the Promised Land

At the conclusion of the forty years in the wilderness, the task of conquering the land confronted the Israelites and Joshua. Scripture records an appearance of the Mal-'akh to Joshua at that time:

> And it came to pass, when Joshua was beside Jericho, that he lifted up his eyes and looked, and, behold, a Man stood opposite him, and His drawn sword was in His hand; and Joshua went to Him, and said to Him, Are You for us, or for our foes? And He said, No, for I now come as the Captain of the army of Jehovah! And Joshua fell on his face to the earth, and worshiped, and said to Him, What does my Lord say to His servant? And the Captain of the army of Jehovah said to Joshua, Take your shoe off your foot, for the place on which you are standing is holy; and Joshua did so.
>
> And Jericho shut itself up, and was barred, because of the presence of the sons of Israel; no one going out, and no one coming in. And Jehovah said to Joshua, See, I have given Jericho and its king, mighty warriors, into your hand. And you shall go around the city, all the men of battle, going around the city once; so you shall do six days; and seven priests shall bear seven trumpets of the jubilee before the ark; and on the seventh day you shall go

around the city seven times, and the priests shall blow with the trumpets; and it shall be, that when they make a long blast with the ram's horn, and when you hear the sound of the horn, all the people shall shout with a great shout; and the wall of the city shall fall down flat; and the people shall go up, each man straight before him. (Joshua 5:13-6:5 Gr.)

The Mal'akh stated that he had given Jericho into the hands of the Israelites and told Joshua how he was to take the city. Only God has such power, yet the Mal'akh claimed such might for himself.

After some years in the Promised Land, the people had become lax and were lapsing into idolatry. We are told that the Mal'akh Jahweh appeared to them in Bochim and rebuked them for their unfaithfulness and disobedience:

The Angel of the LORD came up from Gilgal to Bochim and said: I moved you up out of Egypt, and I have brought you into the land which I promised your fathers by oath, and I said: I will not break My covenant with you through eternity. But you shall make no covenant with the inhabitants of the land; their altars you are to break down. But you have not listened to My voice. What is this you have done? Wherefore I also say to you: I will not drive them out before you; but they shall be your adversaries, and their gods shall be a snare to you. When the Angel of the Lord had spoken these words to all the Israelites, the people lifted up their voices and wept. So they named that place Bochim; and there they sacrificed to the LORD. (Judges 2:1-5 Ber.)

Nowhere in these words did the Mal'akh state that the people had sinned against God, but claimed that the sin was against him. Because of this sin, he declared that he would also punish the people by not allowing them to drive out the heathen nations. As a result of his message the people wept and sacrificed to the Lord. In this passage the Mal'akh claimed the power to judge, to retain and punish the sins of men and to control history. His words moved the people to sacrifice to Jahweh.

Further apostasy resulted in the subjugation of the land by the Midianites. However, when the people turned to God for help the Mal'akh appeared to Gideon. We read of this in the book of Judges. The Mal'akh at this time enabled Gideon to defeat the Midianite host of one hundred thirty-five thousand men with only three hundred men and brought peace and prosperity to his people. Scripture says of this:

> And the Angel of Jehovah came and sat under the oak which is in Ophrah, which belonged to Joash the Abiezrite; and his son Gideon was beating out wheat in the winepress, to hide it from the eyes of the Midianites. And the Angel of Jehovah appeared to him, and said to him, Jehovah is with you, O mighty warrior. And Gideon said to him, O my Lord, if Jehovah is with us, then why has all this happened to us? And where are all His wonders which our fathers recounted to us, saying, Did not Jehovah bring us up out of Egypt? And now Jehovah has left us and has given us into the hands of Midian. And Jehovah turned to him and said, Go in this might of yours and you shall save Israel out of the hand of Midian. Have I not sent you? And he said to him, O my Lord, with what shall I save Israel? Behold, my family is the weakest in Manasseh, and I the least in the house of my father. And Jehovah said to him, Because I am with you, you shall smite the

Midianites as one man. And he said to Him, Please, if I have found grace in Your eyes, then You shall give me a sign that You are speaking with me. Please do not move from here until I come to You and bring my food offering and lay it before You. And He said, I will stay until you come back. And Gideon went in and prepared a kid of the goats, and unleavened bread of an ephah of flour; he put the flesh in a basket, and he put the broth in a pot; and he brought it out to Him, under the oak, and presented it. And the Angel of God said to him, Take the flesh and the unleavened bread and place them on this rock, and pour out the broth. And he did so. And the Angel of Jehovah put forth the end of the staff which was in His hand and touched the flesh and the unleavened bread, and the fire rose up out of the rock and burned up the flesh and the unleavened bread. And the Angel of Jehovah departed out of his sight. And Gideon saw that He was the Angel of Jehovah; and Gideon said, Alas, Lord Jehovah! Because I have seen the Angel of Jehovah face to face! And Jehovah said to him, Peace to you, fear not, you shall not die. And Gideon built an altar to Jehovah there, and called it Jehovahshalom; it is still in Ophrah of the Abiezrites until today. (Judges 6:11-24 Gr.)

More apostasy led to taxation and oppression by the Philistines. After forty years of oppression, God's people undoubtedly yearned and prayed for deliverance. God sent the Mal'akh to announce deliverance to them. We read:

Now a certain man by the name of Manoah, of the tribe of Dan, lived in Zorah. His wife was barren and childless, but the Angel of the LORD appeared to her, and said: See, you have been barren and childless, but you will conceive and bear a son. See that you do not partake of wine or strong drink or any unclean food, for you shall conceive and bear a son. No razor shall touch his head, for he shall be a Nazarite to God from conception. He will begin to rescue Israel out of the hands of the Philistines.

The woman went and told her husband, "A Man of God appeared to me, who had the appearance of the Angel of God, very awe-inspiring. I did not ask Him where He came from, and He did not tell me His name. He said to me: 'See, you have been barren and childless, but now you will conceive and bear a son. You must not partake of wine or strong drink or any unclean food, for he shall be a Nazarite from the time of conception until his death.' "

Then Manoah petitioned the LORD. He said, "Hear me, O LORD! Send the Man of God again to us, that He may instruct us and tell us what we shall do for the child that is to be born." God answered the prayer of Manoah, so that the Angel of God came again to the woman, while she was sitting in the field, her husband not being with her. So the woman ran hurriedly to her husband and said, "Look, the Man who appeared to me the other day has returned." So Manoah got up, followed his wife, and on reaching the Man, inquired, "Are You the Man who spoke to this woman?" The Man said: I am! Then Manoah said, "When what You said comes true, what shall be the lad's way of life and his activities?" The Angel of the LORD said to Manoah: The woman must carry out all my instructions. She must not eat anything made from grapes, nor any unclean thing, nor shall she drink wine or strong drink; all this she must observe. Then Manoah said to the Angel of the LORD, "Please, stay with us; we will kill a kid for You." But the Angel of the Lord said to Manoah: Even though I stay with you, I will not eat of your bread. If you want to, you may offer a burnt offering to the LORD. Manoah did not know that the Man was the Angel of the LORD.

Then Manoah asked the Angel of the LORD, "What is Your name so that we may pay homage to You when Your message comes true?" The Angel of the LORD said: Why do you ask My name, seeing it is Wonderful? Then Manoah offered a kid with a meal offering upon the rock to the LORD, and the Angel did wondrously; Manoah and his wife looked on as the offering was consumed. When the flame went up from the altar toward heaven, the Angel of the LORD ascended in the altar flame. When Manoah and his wife saw this, they threw themselves prone on the ground. But the Angel of the LORD appeared no more to Manoah and his wife. Then Manoah understood that He was the Angel of the LORD.

Manoah said to his wife, "We shall surely die because we have looked upon God." But his wife said, "If the LORD intended to kill us, He would not have accepted a burnt offering and a meal offering from our hands; neither would He have permitted us to see all this or to hear such things as these." (Judges 13:2-23 Ber.)

In these appearances to Manoah and his wife the Mal-'akh announced the birth of Samson, who judged Israel for twenty years, inspiring a fear and dread among the Philistines for his God-given strength and through it, delivering Israel. It is also interesting that when Manoah knew that the messenger whom God had sent to them was the Mal'akh he thought they would die because they had seen God. It is quite evident Manoah and his wife believed in the existence of the Mal'akh and knew he was divine. They found comfort not only in the message they had received but that the Lord had accepted an offering from them.

Later Appearances

It is no wonder that in later years Isaiah spoke of the Angel's great deeds for Israel:

> In all their distress he too was distressed, and the angel of his presence saved them. In his love and mercy he redeemed them; he lifted them up and carried them all the days of old. (Isaiah 63:9 NIV)

Here Isaiah says that the Mal'akh was with his people in their sufferings and saved them. Furthermore, in his love and pity he redeemed them, was patient with them, and carried them all the days of old. It is a picture of the ultimate in love and protection granted any people.

As Isaiah pointed out, the great Mal'akh had carried God's people through the years. His wondrous presence never left them, even during the Babylonian Captivity. In a striking manner a glorious Mal'akh or Messenger saved three of God's faithful believers, and caused King Nebuchadnezzar to honor the true God and his people. Nebuchadnezzar had erected a huge golden image and had commanded all his officials to worship it at a given signal. Three Jews — Shadrach, Meshach and Abednego — refused to do so. As a result, they were thrown into the furnace of execution. Scripture records what happened then:

> And these three men, firmly tied, fell into the blazing furnace. Then King Nebuchadnezzar leaped to his feet in amazement and asked his advisers, "Wasn't it three men

that we tied up and threw into the fire?" They replied,
"Certainly, O king." He said, "Look! I see four men
walking around in the fire, unbound and unharmed, and
the fourth looks like a son of the gods." Nebuchadnezzar
then approached the opening of the blazing furnace and
shouted, "Shadrach, Meshach and Abednego, servants of
the Most High God, come out! Come here!" So Shadrach, Meshach and Abednego came out of the fire, and
the satraps, prefects, governors and royal advisers
crowded around them. They saw that the fire had not
harmed their bodies, nor was a hair of their heads singed;
their robes were not scorched, and there was no smell of
fire on them. Then Nebuchadnezzar said, "Praise be to
the God of Shadrach, Meshach and Abednego, who has
sent his angel and rescued his servants! They trusted in
him and defied the king's command and were willing to
give up their lives rather than serve or worship any god
except their own God. Therefore I decree that the people
of any nation or language who say anything against the
God of Shadrach, Meshach and Abednego be cut into
pieces and their houses be turned into piles of rubble, for
no other god can save in this way."(Daniel 3:23-29 NIV)

Nebuchadnezzar saw a fourth person in the fire with
Shadrach, Meshach, and Abednego. This person had a
divine appearance. And in his presence the fire had no
power over the three men. Nebuchadnezzar, in utter
amazement at him and in admiration for the three men,
summoned them out of the fire. Then the king gave glory
to their God and promoted them in the affairs of Babylon.
He also ordered his entire empire to honor the God of the
Jews; this gave the Jews a more favorable status in the
empire and helped prepare the world for the birth of the
promised Messiah from the Jewish nation. Once again it

seems that it was the Mal'akh who had appeared to help his people. This appearance affected the whole world, not only Babylon. The Mal'akh in this instance used Nebuchadnezzar to glorify God's name throughout the world. Through this God's people were protected and preserved in their captivity.

Sometime later, as the seventy years of captivity were drawing to a close, the great man Daniel was lowered into the den of man-eating lions which was used for executions. He had dared to defy a law which forbade anyone to worship anyone or anything besides the king for thirty days. Scripture describes the event and its result:

> And the king commanded. And they brought Daniel and threw him into the lions' den. The king spoke and said to Daniel, Your God, whom you always serve, will deliver you. And a stone was brought and laid on the mouth of the den. And the king sealed it with his own signet, and with the signet of his nobles, that the affair might not be changed concerning Daniel. Then the king went to his palace and spent the night fasting. And diversions were not brought before him; and his sleep fled from him. Then the king arose in the dawn, in the daylight, and hurried to the lions' den. And when he came to the den, he cried with a grieved voice to Daniel. The king spoke and said to Daniel, O Daniel, servant of the living God, is your God whom you always serve able to deliver you from the lions? Then Daniel said to the king, O king, live forever. My God has sent His Angel, and He has shut the lions' mouths. And they have not hurt me, because in His sight purity was found in me. And also before you, O king, I have done no harm. Then the king was exceedingly happy for him. And he commanded that they should take Daniel up out of the den. So Daniel was taken up out of the den,

and no kind of hurt was found on him, because he trusted in his God. And the king commanded, and they brought those men who had accused Daniel. And they threw them into the lions' den; them, their sons and their wives. And the lions overpowered them and crushed all their bones in pieces before they came to the lower part of the den. Then King Darius wrote to all the peoples, the nations and the languages who were living in all the earth: Peace be multiplied to you. I make a decree that in all my kingdom's domain men shall tremble and fear before the God of Daniel. For He is the living God and endures forever, and His kingdom is the one which shall not be destroyed. And His rule shall be to the end. He delivers and rescues, and He works signs and wonders in the heavens and in the earth, He who has delivered Daniel from the power of the lions. (Daniel 6:16-27 Gr.)

Once again a heaven-sent Mal'akh appeared and before him the fierce lions became gentle. When the king (in this case, a Persian) found Daniel alive the next morning, he had Daniel's foes thrown into the den instead! The king ordered his empire to honor the God of Daniel, the God of the Jews. This assured God's people a better status also under the Persians. The Lord had intervened not only on behalf of Daniel but his people. Through his intervention he both helped the people and also glorified the name of God throughout the world. By once again setting the Jews apart in a special way, the Lord further prepared the way for the Savior.

On another occasion Daniel was granted a glorious vision in which he saw the great Mal'akh in heavenly splendor. The description of the person and glory of the Mal'akh is striking in its similarity to the appearance of

119

the exalted Christ on the Mount of Transfiguration and on the island of Patmos. We find these appearances recorded in Matthew 17:1,2 and in Revelation 1:12-19:

> And after six days Jesus took Peter and James and John, his brother. And he led them into an isolated, high mountain. And He was gloriously changed before them. And His face shone as the sun! And His clothes became white as the light! (Matthew 17:1,2 KJ II)

> And I turned to see the voice which spoke with me. And turning I saw seven golden lampstands. And in the middle of the seven lampstands, I saw One like the Son of man, clothed in a garment reaching to the feet and tied at the breasts with a golden band. And His head and hair were white like wool, like snow. And His eyes were like a flame of fire. And His feet were like fine brass, as if made to glow in a furnace. And His voice was like the voice of many waters. And He had seven stars in His right hand and a sharp two-edged sword going forth out of His mouth. And His face was as the sun shines in its power. And when I saw Him, I fell at His feet as dead. And He laid His right hand on me, saying to me, Do not fear. I am the First and the Last and the Living One. And I became dead, and, Look! I am alive forever and ever. Amen. And I have the keys of hell and of death. Write the things which you saw, and the things which are, and the things which are going to take place after these things. (Revelation 1:12-19 KJ II)

In Daniel 10:4-11:1 we read:

> And in the twenty-fourth day of the first month, as I was by the side of the great river, which is Tigris, then I lifted up my eyes and looked. And, behold, a certain man was clothed in linen, whose loins were wrapped in fine gold from Uphaz. His body also was like the beryl, and his face looked like lightning. And his eyes were like lamps of fire, and his arms and his feet in color were like polished

copper, and the voice of his words as the sound of a multitude. And I, Daniel, alone saw the vision. For the men who were with me did not see the vision. But a great quaking fell on them, so that they fled to hide themselves. Then I was left alone and saw this great vision, and there remained no strength in me. For my beauty was turned within me to corruption, and I kept no strength. Yet I heard the voice of his words. And when I heard the voice of his words, then I was in a deep sleep on my face, and my face was toward the ground. And, behold, a hand touched me and set me on my knees and the palms of my hands. And he said to me, O Daniel, a man greatly beloved, understand the words that I speak to you and stand up. For to you I am now sent. And when he had spoken this word to me, I stood trembling. Then he said to me, Do not fear, Daniel, for from the first day that you set your heart to understand and to chasten yourself before your God, your words were heard. And I have come for your words. But the prince of the kingdom of Persia withstood me twenty-one days. But, lo, Michael, one of the leading rulers, came to help me. And I stayed there with the kings of Persia. Now I have come to make you understand what shall happen to your people in the latter days. For the vision is yet for many days. And when he had spoken such words to me, I bowed my face to the ground and I became dumb. And, behold, one looking like the sons of men touched my lips. Then I opened my mouth and spoke and said to him who stood before me, My lord, my pangs have stricken me, because of the vision, and I have no strength left. For how can the servant of my lord talk to you? For as for me, there is no power left in me; yea, there is no breath left in me. Then again one looking like a man came and touched me, and he made me stronger. And he said, O man greatly loved, do not fear. Peace to you. Be strong. Yes, be strong. And when he had spoken to me, I was made stronger. And I said, Speak, my lord, for you have made me stronger. Then he said, Do you know why I come to you? And now I will return to fight with the king of Persia. And when I have gone out, lo, the king of Greece shall come. But I will show you that which is written in the Scripture of Truth. And no one holds strongly with me in these things except Michael your prince. Also in the first year of Darius the Mede, I, even I, stood to establish and to strengthen him. (KJ II)

The glory and majesty of the Mal'akh in these passages of Scripture is so great that it cannot possibly refer to a created angel. Such a glory belongs to only one Angel, the Mal'akh Jahweh.

The Mal'akh at this time is sent by God to reveal to Daniel what he had been seeking in prayer and fasting. The Angel revealed that he was contending with the evil and stubborn spirit influencing the kings of Persia, and that he had called upon the Archangel Michael to help him in this matter. Michael is pictured in Scripture as the war angel or the protecting angel of God's people, the leader of the angel army of heaven. The superiority of the Mal'akh to Michael can be seen in the fact that the Mal'akh had summoned Michael to serve him in his work of judgment upon Persia. This can again be seen in Daniel 11:1, where the Mal'akh says that he confirmed and strengthened Michael in the days of Darius the Mede.

Daniel's reaction is the same as that of John on the island of Patmos. At the awesome sight of the Mal'akh, Daniel fell to the ground as a dead man. He was rendered breathless and powerless. He was so overcome that he gasped, "How can the servant of my Lord talk to you? For as for me there is no breath left in me." In order even to function Daniel needs strengthening from the Mal'akh.

Here we see the Mal'akh guiding world events for his people. He is the victor over the forces of Satan, the Lord of history and the Lord of the angels of heaven. Divine glory, power and dominion belong to him. What a comfort it must have been for Daniel to see that he and his people rested in the Mal'akh's hands! What a comfort and joy it should be for all who are God's people — today, tomorrow and forever!

It is only natural that Malachi, the last prophet of the Old Testament, speaks of the Mal'akh as the promised Messiah. It should be noted that Malachi refers to two coming messengers. One was the herald; this was John the Baptist. The second was the Messiah or Christ. Speaking through Malachi, the Lord declares:

> "*I am going to send My messenger to prepare a way for Me.* And the LORD whom you're looking for will suddenly come to His temple, yes, the Angel of the covenant whom you delight in — He will come, "says the LORD of armies. But when He comes, *who can bear it?* When He shows Himself, *who can stand it?* He is like a refiner's fire, like cleaners' soap. And He will sit down like one who refines and cleanses silver to cleanse Levi's descendants and purify them like gold and silver. Then they will in a righteous way bring offerings to the LORD. (Malachi 3:1-3 AAT)

The Mal'akh had played a tremendous and well-known role in Old Testament Jewish history. So great had his role been that he was looked upon by the believing Jews as their Savior. Malachi gives expression to this belief and caps it when he says that the Mal'akh of the covenant, in whom the Jews of his day delighted, would be the one whom God would send on the Messianic mission of salvation to the world.

The Mal'akh's Power of Divine Judgment

Today we often speak of sin and sinners and of God's impending judgment. We have this knowledge because of what the Bible says.

In the New Testament we read:

> "Why does He talk this way? It is blasphemy. Who but God alone can forgive sins?" (Mark 2:7 Ber.)

> And the scribes and the Pharisees began to question, saying, Who is this who speaks blasphemies? Who is able to forgive sins except God alone? (Luke 5:21 KJ II)

According to these passages even Jesus' enemies recognized that God alone has the power to forgive sins. In 1 John, we learn that sin is the transgression of the Law:

> Everyone who sins breaks the Law. Sin is breaking the Law. (1 John 3:4 AAT)

In the book of Ecclesiastes we are told that all people sin:

> For there is not one righteous man on earth who does good and never sins. (Ecclesiastes 7:20 Ber.)

The basic truth of man's sinfulness before the holy God was derived from the Old Testament by the Jews at the time of Christ. It was also a truth known to the Old Testament Jews. We note this in a number of passages:

> You shall not bow yourself down to them or serve them. For I the Lord your God am a jealous God, visiting the iniquity of the fathers on the children to the third and

fourth generation of those that hate Me, and showing mercy to thousands of those that love Me and keep My commandments. (Exodus 20:5,6 KJ II)

"When they sin against you — for there is no one who does not sin — and you become angry with them and give them over to the enemy, who takes them captive to his own land, far away or near; and if they have a change of heart in the land where they are held captive, and repent and plead with you in the land of their conquerors and say, 'We have sinned, we have done wrong, we have acted wickedly'; and if they turn back to you with all their heart and soul in the land of their enemies who took them captive, and pray to you toward the land you gave their fathers, toward the city you have chosen and the temple I have built for your Name; then from heaven, your dwelling place, hear their prayer and their plea, and uphold their cause. And forgive your people, who have sinned against you; forgive all the offenses they have committed against you, and cause their conquerors to show them mercy; for they are your people and your inheritance, whom you brought out of Egypt, out of that iron-smelting furnace." (1 Kings 8:46-51 NIV)

God's Old Testament people were very conscious of sin and the judgment of God upon sin. The histories of the Fall and the Flood portrayed this truth very vividly.

But the believers lived in a world which refused to remember the true God and his Word. Because the world was so evil God chose to build a nation which would be the cradle of the Savior. The story of the building of this Messianic people and the fulfillment of the promise of the Messiah's birth is the most beautiful story of all time.

As part of this magnificent story, one of the great fascinations of the Old Testament is the story of him who shaped God's people, who defended God's people, who was born to save the world, namely, the Mal'akh Jahweh of the Old Testament. His power over history and nations makes one stand and marvel. His power of divine judgment is awesome and makes one tremble.

As we survey the history of God's Old Testament people from the time of Abraham we can see a series of tremendous judgments carried out by the Mal'akh of God, also called the Destroyer. Some feel that various created angels were sent by God to perform these tasks. The author feels that they bear the mark of one divine Being, that of the Mal'akh Jahweh.

Judgment upon Sodom

The first instance of the divine power of the Mal'akh for judgment is found in Genesis 18 and 19. Here we are told of Abraham's prayer for Sodom and of the destruction of the evil cities. We note that God and two messengers appeared in human form to Abraham and Sarah. Scripture indicates that Abraham and Sarah knew they were heavenly beings:

> And Jehovah appeared to him [Abraham] by the oaks of Mamre; and he sat at the tent door in the heat of the day. And he lifted up his eyes and looked; and lo, three men stood facing him. And when he saw them, he ran from the tent door to meet them; and he bowed himself toward the ground. And he said, My Lord, if I have now found favor in Your sight, I beg You, do not leave Your servant. I beg You, let a little water be brought, and wash Your feet, and rest under the tree. And I will bring a bite of bread, and You may strengthen Your heart; then You may go on, for

this is why You have come to Your servant. And they said, Do so, as you have said. (Genesis 18:1-5 Gr.)

That Abraham knew that his guest was God himself we learn from his prayer for Sodom:

And Jehovah said, Shall I hide from Abraham the thing which I do, when Abraham shall surely become a great and powerful nation, and all the nations of the earth shall be blessed him? For I have known him, in order that he may command his sons and his house after him; and that they may observe the way of Jehovah, to do righteousness and judgment, in order that Jehovah may bring on Abraham that which He has spoken of him. And Jehovah said, Because the cry of Sodom and Gomorrah is great, and because their sin is very heavy, I will go down now and see whether they have done altogether according to the cry that comes to Me; and if not, I will know. And the men turned their faces away from there and went toward Sodom; and Abraham was still standing before Jehovah. And Abraham came near and said, Will You even sweep away the righteous with the wicked? Perhaps there are fifty righteous within the city; will You even sweep away, not sparing the place for the fifty righteous that are in it? Far be it from You to act in this way, to kill the righteous with the wicked. And far be it from You, that the righteous should be as the wicked. Shall not the Judge of all the earth do right? And Jehovah said, If I find fifty righteous in Sodom, within the city, then I will spare all the place for their sakes. And Abraham answered and said, Behold, now, I have undertaken to speak to the Lord, I who am dust and ashes. Perhaps there will be five lacking from the fifty righteous; will You destroy all the city for five? And He said, If I find forty-five there, I will not destroy it. And he continued still to speak to Him and said, Perhaps forty will be found there. And He said, I will not do it for the sake of forty. And he said, Do not let the Lord be angry now, that I may speak; perhaps there will be thirty found. And He said, I will not do it if I find thirty there. And he said, Behold, now, I have undertaken to speak to the Lord; perhaps twenty will be found there. And He said, I will not destroy it for the sake of the twenty. And he said, Do not let the Lord be angry now, that I may speak this time only; perhaps ten will be found there. And He said, I will not destroy for the sake of the ten. (Genesis 18:17-32 Gr.)

In Genesis 19 we read that the two "angels" arrived in Sodom and were invited by Lot to spend the night in his home. When the homosexual men of the city sought to force Lot to surrender them, they blinded the crowd and warned Lot and his family to leave before dawn when the city would be destroyed.

Lot warned his married daughters and their husbands but the husbands laughed. Finally the mal'akhs dragged Lot and his wife and unmarried daughters to the city gates and warned them to flee to the mountains and not look back. Lot then said to these mal'akhs:

Oh no, Lord, behold now, Your servant has found grace in Your sight, and You have magnified Your mercy which You have shown to me in saving my life; and I cannot escape to the mountain, lest some evil take me and I die. Behold, now, this city is near to flee to, and it is a little one. Oh let me escape there, it being a little thing, that my soul may live. (Genesis 19:18-20 Gr.)

The one Mal'akh replied:

See, I have accepted your face for this thing also, without overthrowing the city for which you have spoken. Hurry, escape there, for I am not able to do anything until you have come there; so the name of the city was called Zoar. (Genesis 19:21,22 Gr.)

Lot and his family ran to Zoar according to the word of the Angel. Scripture declares:

> The sun had risen on the earth, and Lot entered into Zoar. And Jehovah rained brimstone and fire on Sodom and on Gomorrah, from Jehovah, out of the heavens. And He overthrew the cities, and all the plain, and all the inhabitants of the cities, and that which grew out of the ground. And his wife looked back, from behind him, and she became a pillar of salt. (Genesis 19:23-26 Gr.)

This is the first instance in which God used his Mal'akh in a punitive or judgmental role. From the words of the story the one Mal'akh held the power of judgment in his hands. He claimed the power to spare Zoar for Lot's sake. He said he could do nothing until Lot had escaped. Then Scripture says that Jehovah destroyed the entire plain. Throughout the Old Testament the power of judgment is reserved for God. Here the Mal'akh claims it is his and then carries it out. Such an awesome display of divine power in the Old Testament is normal only to the divinely sent Destroyer or Angel of God. His acts of Judgment affect nations and the earth itself. Nowhere do created angels display this type of power or authority. To the Mal'akh it was normal.

Judgment upon Egypt

We again see the awesome punitive and judgmental power of the Mal'akh during the tenth plague in Egypt. God had virtually destroyed Egypt through nine plagues and thus rendered it powerless to harm his departing people. God announced that in the tenth plague they would be set free. Believing this promise, some 2,000,000 Israelites gathered behind doors whose lintels and posts were marked by the blood of a lamb which had been killed and roasted whole for the first Passover meal. They were eating it in haste, ready to march. This was the night of their deliverance through God's Mal'akh. All the first-born in Egypt of man and beast would die. But the Israelites would be safe, because God had said through Moses:

> And Jehovah will pass through to smite Egypt; and He will see the blood on the lintel and on the two side door-posts; and Jehovah will pass over the door, and He will not allow the destroyer to come into your house to strike you. (Exodus 12:23 Gr.)

As God had promised, his Destroyer, the Mal'akh, went out over Egypt and killed every firstborn of man and beast. He spared only the houses which were marked by the blood of the lamb. The scale of the judgment was awesome. It was done to deliver God's people. This role of Deliverer, Protector and Guide of God's people was the great role of the Mal'akh throughout the Old Testament. It would seem that this was the second of his great punitive dealings with men.

God's love for his people and the Mal'akh's awesome punitive power in defending those people were again demonstrated as the Israelites left the borders of Egypt. As they left Egypt, they did not leave with Moses as their only visible guide and defender. Scripture tells us that Jehovah led them in a pillar of cloud by day and a pillar of fire by night. During the day they followed the pillar of cloud and at night they moved about and slumbered in its light. This cloud never left them in their journey to the Promised Land.

It is interesting to note that whereas in Exodus 13, the Lord is in the cloud, in chapter 14, the Angel of the Lord is in the cloud. First he is referred to as Jehovah and then as the Mal'akh, thus demonstrating that he was divine, a separate person in the Godhead.

It should also be noted here that he never left God's people. He was always present in the cloud. What comfort and joy he brought to God's people by his mighty presence!

He first demonstrated this by moving between his people and the Egyptian army at the Red Sea. He enveloped the Egyptians in darkness from the one side of the cloud and rendered them helpless. He gave his people light for their passage through the sea from the other side of the cloud.

In the morning we are told that he looked from the cloud upon the Egyptians. Again he is called Jehovah. He then let the Egyptian army see the path through the Red Sea. When they entered it, he caused the waters to return and drown the entire army. The Mal'akh thus completed the destruction of Egypt as a world power and rendered them incapable of harming Israel during the forty years in the wilderness:

> And Jehovah was going before them by day in a pillar of cloud, to lead them in the way; and by night in a pillar of fire, to give light to them, to go by day and by night. The pillar of cloud did not cease by day, and the pillar of fire by night, before the people. (Exodus 13:21,22 Gr.)

And the Angel of God withdrew, the One going before the camp of Israel, and He went behind them, and the pillar of cloud withdrew from before them, and it stood behind them. And it came between the camp of Egypt and the camp of Israel; and it was cloudy and dark, and it gave light to the night; and this one did not come near to that one all night.

And Moses stretched out his hand over the sea, and Jehovah caused the sea to go back by a strong east wind all night; and He made the sea dry land, and the waters were divided. And the children of Israel came into the middle of the sea on dry ground, the waters being a wall to them from their right hand and from their left hand. And the Egyptians pursued, and all the horses of Pharaoh came after them, his chariots and his horsemen, into the middle of the sea. And it happened in the morning watch, Jehovah looked on the camp of the Egyptians in the pillar of fire and cloud; and He confused the camp of the Egyptians. (Exodus 14:19-24 Gr.)

Judgments Upon Israel

With the establishment of the kingdom under David and the growth of the school of prophets, the Mal'akh appeared visibly only once in a punitive role. Israel had angered God and David their king had committed the sin of pride in having his subjects counted. Scripture says of this:

And the king said to Joab, the captain of the host that was with him, Go now to and fro through all the tribes of Israel, from Dan even to Beersheba, and number the people, that I may know the sum of the people. And Joab said to the king, Yea, may Jehovah your God add to the people, however many they may be, a hundredfold, and may the eyes of my lord the king see it; but why does my lord the king delight in this thing? But the word of the king prevailed against Joab, and against the captains of the army; and Joab went out, and the captains of the army from the presence of the king, to muster the people, even Israel. And they crossed over the Jordan and camped in Aroer, on the right side of the city that is in the middle of the valley of Gad, and to Jazer; and they came into Gilead, and to the land of Tahtimhodshi; and they came to Dan-jann, and around to Sidon. And they came into the fortress of Tyre, and all the cities of the Hivite, and of the Canaanite, and went out to the south of Judah, to Beersheba. And they went to and fro through all the land, and came in at the end of nine months and twenty days to Jerusalem. And Joab gave the count from the mustering of the people to the king; and Israel was eight hundred thousand mighty men drawing sword, and the men of Judah five hundred thousand men.

And the heart of David smote him, after he had numbered the people; and David said to Jehovah, I have sinned greatly in that which I have done, and now, O Jehovah, I beg of You, cause the iniquity of your servant to pass away, for I have done very foolishly. And David rose up in the morning, and the word of Jehovah came to Gad the prophet, the seer of David, saying, Go, and you shall speak to David, Thus says Jehovah, I am setting up three things for you; you choose one of them, and I will do it to you. And Gad came in to David and told him, and said to him, Shall seven years of famine come to you in your land; or shall you flee before your adversaries three months, and he pursue you; or shall three days' plague come into your land? Now consider and see what word I shall take back to Him who sent me. And David said to Gad, I am in great distress; let us fall now into the hand of Jehovah, for many are His mercies; and do not let me fall into the hand of man.

And Jehovah sent a plague upon Israel from the morning

even to the time appointed, and from Dan even to Beersheba seventy-thousand men of the people died. And the angel put forth his hand to Jerusalem to destroy it, and Jehovah repented as to the evil and said to the angel who was destroying among the people, Enough! Now stop your hand. And the angel of Jehovah was near the threshing-floor of Araunah the Jebusite. And David spoke to Jehovah, when he saw the angel who was smiting among the people, and said, Behold, I have sinned! Yea, I have acted perversely; and these, the flock, what have they done? Let now Your hand be upon me, and on the house of my father.

And Gad came in to David on that day, and said to him, Go up, raise an altar to Jehovah in the threshing-floor of Araunah the Jebusite. And David went up according to the word of Gad, as Jehovah commanded. And Araunah looked and saw the king and his servants crossing over to him; and Araunah went out and bowed himself to the king, his face to the earth to the king. And Araunah said, Why has my lord the king come to his servant? And David said, To buy the threshing-floor from you, to build an altar to Jehovah, and the plague shall be stayed from the people. (2 Samuel 24:2-21 Gr.)

In 1 Chronicles we also read about this event:

And God sent an angel to Jerusalem to destroy it; and as he was destroying, Jehovah saw, and was comforted as to the evil, and said to the angel who was destroying, Enough! Now stay your hand. And the angel of Jehovah stood by the threshing-floor or Ornan the Jebusite. And David lifted up his eyes and saw the angel of Jehovah standing between the earth and the heavens, and his sword drawn in his hand, stretched out over Jerusalem; and David and the elders fell down on their faces, covered with sackcloth. And David said to God, Was it not I, I who said to number the people? Yea, it was I who sinned, and have done great evil; and these, the flock, what have they done? O Jehovah, my God, I pray You, let Your hand be on me and on the house of my father, and not on Your people, to be plagued.

And the angel of Jehovah spoke to Gad, saying to David, Surely David shall go up to raise an altar to Jehovah in the threshing-floor of Ornan the Jebusite. And David went up by the word of Gad, that which he spoke in the name of Jehovah. And Ornan turned back, and saw the angel; and his four sons that were with him hid themselves; and Ornan was threshing wheat. And as David came to Ornan, Ornan looked and saw David, and went out of the threshing-floor and bowed down to David, with his face to the ground. And David said to Ornan, Give me the site of the threshing-floor, and I will build an altar to Jehovah in it; for full price give it to me, and the plague will be restrained from the people. And Ornan said to David, Take it for yourself, and my lord the king do that which is good in his eyes; see, I have given the oxen for burnt offerings, and the threshing instruments for wood, and the wheat for the food offering; I give it all. And King David said to Ornan, No, for I will surely buy it for full price; for I will not offer that which is yours to Jehovah, so as to offer a burnt offering without cost. And David gave to Ornan six hundred shekels of gold in weight for the place. And David built an altar there to Jehovah, and offered burnt offerings and peace offerings, and called to Jehovah; and He answered him with fire from the heavens on the altar of the burnt offering. And Jehovah commanded the angel, and he returned his sword to its sheath.

At that time, when David saw that Jehovah had answered him in the threshing-floor of Ornan the Jebusite, then he sacrificed there. And the tabernacle of Jehovah that Moses had made in the wilderness, and the altar of burnt offering, were at that time in the high place in Gibeon; and David was not able to go before it to seek God, for he was afraid because of the sword of the angel of Jehovah. (1 Chronicles 21:15-30 Gr.)

God through his prophet Gad let David choose one of three punishments: famine, defeat or a plague from God. David chose to fall into the hands of God because of his great mercy. God's judgment was swift and awesome. He sent the Mal'akh over the land as he had sent him many years earlier in Egypt.

Seventy thousand people died throughout the land, and as the Mal'akh Jahweh was approaching Jerusalem to destroy it, David went with the elders of Israel to the threshing-floor of Ornan, also called Araunah, the Jebusite. There they fell down before the visible Mal'akh. Scripture says that David pleaded with God for the life of his people. In humble penitence David asked that the punishment might fall on him instead.

In answer to David's prayer, the Mal'akh instructed the prophet Gad to tell David to offer a burnt offering at the threshing-floor of Ornan the Jebusite. David did so and the offering was devoured by fire from heaven. One cannot help noting how remarkably similar this is to the times when the Mal'akh accepted offerings from Gideon and Manoah. They offered sacrifices at his word and each sacrifice was consumed in flame. When the offering had been given, God ordered the Mal'akh to cease his destruction.

Some facts need to be reviewed in this appearance of the Mal'akh. The Mal'akh was seen by David and the elders of Israel. When he was seen, David prayed to God. He was also seen by Ornan and the sons of Ornan. The sacrifice was devoured in divine flame. The Mal'akh was stopped on his mission of destruction by Jahweh or Elohim. The Mal'akh, then, is shown to be divine, yet a separate person in the Godhead.

The book of 2 Chronicles refers back to this incident and definitely calls the Mal'akh God, when it says that Solomon built the temple where Jahweh appeared to David in the threshing-floor of Ornan the Jebusite:

> And Solomon began to build the house of Jehovah at Jerusalem, in Mount Moriah, where He appeared to his father David, in the place that David had prepared, in the threshing-floor of Ornan the Jebusite. (2 Chronicles 3:1 Gr.)

There can be no doubt that David knew the Mal'akh and looked upon him as the defender of God's people. We can see this in Psalms 34 and 35. In Psalm 34 David praises God for saving him from his foes. He notes that God's people had always been saved by God. As David thinks of God's wondrous protection, he sees the divine Mal'akh enfolding God's people and surrounding them with his mighty presence as he did during the exodus from Egypt:

> The angel of the LORD encamps around those who fear him, and he delivers them. (Psalm 34:7 NIV)

It is simply beautiful to note with David that the Mal'akh envelopes and surrounds those who *fear* him, that is, those who believe in him and own him as their Savior, their Deliverer, their Protector. Who then can harm God's people?

It is also important to note that David says that the

Mal'akh envelopes and protects those who fear *him*. This definitely refers to worship being extended to the Mal-'akh. Worship is always reserved for God alone. David speaks of the Mal'akh as divine and yet as a separate person in the Godhead.

In Psalm 35 we again see that David knew the Mal'akh and his role as God's divine Messenger. David also expressed his belief in the power of the Mal'akh for judgment when he prayed God to send the Mal'akh to pursue his enemies:

> May they be like chaff before the wind, with the angel of the LORD driving them away; may their path be dark and slippery, with the angel of the LORD pursuing them. (Psalm 35:5,6 NIV)

Not only does David pray that the Mal'akh would pursue his enemies, but that he would also cause them to fall and that he would punish them. The Mal'akh, so to speak, was to be David's avenger against the ungodly. Certainly such power belongs to God alone.

Solomon, David's son, shows this still more clearly when he says in the book of Ecclesiastes:

> When you vow to God, don't delay to pay it because he doesn't like fools. Pay what you vow. Better not vow than vow and not pay it. Don't let your mouth get you into sin or say before the angel, "It was a mistake." Why should God get angry with what you say and destroy what you've done. (Ecclesiastes 5:4-6 AAT)

Here he urges believers to be careful in their speech, lest evil speech cause them to commit sinful acts. Moreover, if a believer should fall into such sin, he should not be brazen and try to excuse himself before the Mal'akh by claiming it to be a mistake. Such an attitude would incur the anger of God and lead to judgment and condemnation. The Mal'akh is pictured as being the Judge of man's sins and if he is sinned against, God is sinned against.

This power of the Mal'akh to judge, to condemn and to destroy is again clearly shown in 2 Kings 1:

And Ahaziah fell through the lattice in his upper room that was in Samaria, and was sick, and sent messengers and said to them, Go, ask of Baalzebub the god of Ekron if I will recover from this sickness. And an angel of Jehovah spoke to Elijah the Tishbite, Rise, Go up to meet the messengers of the king of Samaria, and say to them, Is it because there is not a God in Israel that you are going to ask of Baalzebub the god of Ekron? And therefore, so says Jehovah, You shall not come down from that bed on which you have gone up, but you shall surely die. And Elijah departed. And the messengers returned to him, and he said to them, What is this, that you have turned back? And they said to him, A man came up to meet us, and said to us, Go, return to the king who sent you; and you shall say to him, So says Jehovah, Is it because there is not a God in Israel that you are sending to ask of Baalzebub the god of Ekron? Therefore, you shall not come down from the bed on which you have gone up, for you shall certainly die. And he said to them, What was the fashion of the man who came up to meet you and spoke these words to you? And they said to him, A hairy man, and a girdle of leather was girded about his loins. And he said, He is Elijah the Tishbite. And the king sent to him the captain of fifty with his fifty; and he went up to him — and behold, he was sitting on the top of the hill —and he spoke to him, O man of God, the king has said, Come down. And Elijah answered and said to the captain of the fifty, And if I am a man of God, fire shall come down from the heavens and shall consume you and your fifty. And fire came down from the heavens and consumed him and his fifty. And he turned and sent another head of fifty and his fifty to him; and he answered and said to him, O man of God, thus says the king, Hurry, come down. And Elijah answered and said to them, If I am a man of God, fire shall come down from the heavens and shall consume you and your fifty. And fire from God came down from the heavens and consumed him and his fifty.

And he turned and sent a third captain of fifty and his fifty; and the third captain of fifty went up, and came and fell on his knees before Elijah, and begged him, and said to him, O man of God, please let my soul and the soul of your servants, these fifty, be precious in your eyes. Behold, fire has come down from the heavens and has consumed the two captains of the former fifties and their fifties; and, now, let my soul be precious in your eyes. And the Angel of Jehovah spoke to Elijah, Go down with him; do not be afraid of him. And he rose and went down with him to the king. And he said to him, So says Jehovah, Because you have sent messengers to ask of Baalzebub the god of Ekron, is it because there is not a God in Israel to inquire of His word? Therefore, you shall not come down from the bed on which you have gone up, for you shall certainly die. And he died, according to the word of Jehovah that Elijah spoke. And Jehoram reigned in his place, in the second year of Jehoram the son of Jehoshaphat, the king of Judah, for he had no sons. (2 Kings 1:2-17 Gr.)

Ahaziah, the ungodly king of the Northern Kingdom of Israel, followed in the sins of his father Ahab. This angered God. After a two year reign, Ahaziah fell and critically injured himself. Instead of asking the God of Israel for help and guidance, he sent a delegation to seek the counsel of Baalzebub of Ekron, "the god of flies."

Scripture declares that the Mal'akh Jahweh ordered Elijah to intercept Ahaziah's delegation and to send it back to Ahaziah with a message of condemnation and death for his unbelief.

Ahaziah ordered his troops to bring Elijah to him. Three squads of fifty men were sent out. The first two were belligerent, unbelieving and potentially harmful to Elijah. As a tool of divine judgment Elijah called down fire from heaven upon the first two squads and destroyed them.

The last squad approached in humility and fear and a belief that God was displaying divine power and judgment through Elijah. The captain prayed for mercy.

The Mal'akh then instructed Elijah to accompany the squad. He did so and pronounced God's judgment of death upon Ahaziah. It is significant to note that the Mal'akh guided and controlled the entire situation. Elijah was only his spokesman. Here again we see the great Mal'akh judging and condemning for sin. He shows he has the power of life and death; he defends his people and destroys their foes.

Judgment and Forgiveness

The power of the Mal'akh in the defense of God's people and his judgment on their foes was again vividly demonstrated when Sennacherib, the proud king of Assyria, thought he would destroy Jerusalem. He sent a blasphemous letter to king Hezekiah and demanded his surrender. Hezekiah took the letter to the temple, spread it out before God and prayed for help. God sent the prophet Isaiah to comfort the king and to assure him of God's help. Scripture describes the help God sent in the book of 2 Kings:

> That night the angel of the LORD went out and put to death a hundred and eighty-five thousand men in the Assyrian camp. When the people got up the next morning —there were all the dead bodies! So Sennacherib king of Assyria broke camp and withdrew. He returned to Nineveh and stayed there. (2 Kings 19:35,36 NIV)

As God promised, no harm came to his people. He sent the great Mal'akh to destroy the Assyrian army and deliver his people. And once again the Mal'akh displayed his awesome might.

Not only were human beings subject to the Mal'akh but also the angels of heaven. Not only did he seek the welfare of God's people by might but also through prayer. The prophet Zechariah sets this before us when he says:

> On the twenty-fourth day of the eleventh month, which is the month Shebat, in the second year of Darius, the word of the LORD came to Zechariah, the son of Berechiah, the son of Iddo the prophet, saying, I watched by night. And, behold! A Man riding on a red horse. And he stood among the myrtle trees that were in the shade. And behind Him were red, sorrel and white horses. Then I said, O my lord, what are these? And the angel who talked with me said to me, I will show you what these are. And the Man who stood among the myrtle trees answered and said, These are those whom the LORD has sent to walk to and fro through the earth. And they answered the Angel of the LORD who stood among the myrtle trees and said, We

have walked to and fro through the earth, and, behold, all the earth sits still and is at rest. Then the Angel of the LORD answered and said, O LORD of hosts, how long will You not have mercy on Jerusalem and on the cities of Judah, against which You have had fury these seventy years? And the LORD answered the angel who talked with me with good words and comfortable words. (Zechariah 1:7-13 KJ II)

Being guided by an angel, the prophet here sees the Mal'akh as the one who sends the angels of God on their missions and receives their account when they return. Zechariah hears him pray for God's people for an end to their punishment in the captivity. In beautiful and comforting words which Zechariah is to proclaim, God responds.

The Mal'akh is shown to be Lord over the angels and to be the Intercessor for God's people. It is one of Christ's roles which we rejoice in as God's New Testament Christians. Little wonder the Old Testament believers loved and revered the Mal'akh.

Even Satan acknowledges the power of the Mal'akh to judge and to forgive sins. Scripture expresses this, saying:

And He showed me Joshua the high priest standing before the Angel of Jehovah, and Satan standing at his right hand to accuse him. And Jehovah said to Satan, Jehovah rebuke you, Satan! And, Jehovah who has chosen Jerusalem rebuke you! Is this not a brand plucked out of the fire? Now Joshua was clothed with filthy clothes, and he stood before the Angel. And He answered and spoke to those who stood before Him, saying, Take away the filthy clothes from him. And to him He said, Behold, I have caused your iniquity to pass from you, and I will clothe you with costly robes. And I said, Let them set a clean turban on his head. So they set a clean turban on his head and clothed him with clothing. And the Angel of Jehovah stood by. And the Angel of Jehovah admonished Joshua, saying, Thus says Jehovah of hosts: If you will walk in My ways, and if you will keep My charge, then you shall also judge My house and shall also keep My courts, and I will give you room to walk among these who stand by. (Zechariah 3:1-7 Gr.)

Here Joshua, the high priest, is pictured as standing before the Mal'akh Jahweh for judgment while Satan stands by as the accuser. Although Joshua is spoken of as being before the Mal'akh, we are also told that it is Jahweh who addresses Satan and rebukes him, stating that Joshua is a brand plucked from the fire. He then orders the angels to remove the filthy garb of Joshua and to clothe him with heavenly clothing. The scene is definitely one in which Joshua is granted forgiveness and righteousness by the Mal'akh. The term Mal'akh Jahweh is changed to Jahweh when he speaks and yet the same Being is addressing Satan and Joshua. Here, then, the Mal'akh is pictured as having power to sit in judgment, to forgive sins, to make Satan bow before him, and to make good angels do his bidding.

As we consider the power of judgment the Mal'akh possessed, the question of the Pharisees in Mark 2:7 and Luke 5:21 becomes extremely relevant, "Who can forgive sins but God?" The Mal'akh could and did.

Christ as the
Angel of the Lord

Savior

Prince of Heaven

Burning Bush

Judge

Pillar of
Cloud and Fire

Divine Messenger

Warrior

Avenging Angel

The Divine Person
and Mission of the Mal'akh Jahweh

The Mal'akh as God

When the Mal'akh appeared to people in the Old Testament they were left with the positive conviction that they had seen and talked with God. The first reference to the Mal'akh Jahweh is found in Genesis 16:7, as we noted earlier. Sarah had grown weary of waiting for God to grant her a son and had resorted to the custom of giving her maid to her husband as a concubine. Any offspring the wife could claim as her own. Sarah's maid Hagar became pregnant and openly showed contempt for her. Consequently Sarah appealed to Abraham and, once given a free hand, drove Hagar away with harsh treatment. While she was resting near a spring, the Mal'akh appeared to Hagar and gently chided her for running away. He then commanded her to return, promising to bless her and her son. While we are told that the Mal'akh appeared to her and spoke to her, he is designated later as Jahweh by the writer. Hagar herself called him Elohim, the name for God, meaning the high, mighty God. She said, "Thou Elohim art my Beholder or Seer." Thus the Mal'akh is here separate from God in person, yet God himself.

As we saw in Genesis 22, after Sarah finally did have a son Abraham was instructed by God to take Isaac and sacrifice him on a designated mountain. Abraham set out in unquestioning faith to carry out God's command. When he had built the altar and arranged the wood, he placed Isaac upon it. Abraham was about to kill his only son when suddenly the voice of the Mal'akh Jahweh stopped him, saying, "Now I know that thou fearest God, seeing thou hast not withheld thy Son, thine only son from me." The Mal'akh said Isaac had not been withheld from him. The honor of sacrifice God reserved only for himself in the Old Testament. Abraham had been ready to sacrifice Isaac to the Mal'akh. The Mal'akh then blessed Abraham and provided a ram for Abraham to offer to Jahweh as a thank offering. Abraham was convinced the Mal'akh was God and named that never-to-be-forgotten hill, Jehovah-jireh, meaning "At the hill of Jahweh" or "The Lord will provide." He refers to the Mal'akh as Jahweh and names the hill after his mercy.

Possibly the man who had the closest and most frequent contact with the Mal'akh was Jacob. On his deathbed he prayed over his grandsons Ephraim and Manasseh:

> God, before whom my fathers Abraham and Isaac did walk, the God which fed me all my life long unto this day, the Angel which redeemed me from all evil, bless the lads; and let my name be named on them, and the name of my fathers Abraham and Isaac; and let them grow into a multitude in the midst of the earth. (Genesis 48:15,16 KJV)

In this blessing Jacob refers to the God of his fathers as the God who had sustained him. He then refers to the Angel separately as the One who had redeemed him from all evil. He prayed the Mal'akh to permit the name of Israel to be named on his half-Egyptian grandsons, that they might share in the blessings of God's chosen people. He thus distinguished between God and the Mal'akh —the Mal'akh being separate in person, yet God himself.

It is interesting to note in this connection that years before Abraham and Eliezer, his foreman, spoke of God's Angel in a similar way. Abraham instructed his servant:

> "The LORD, the God of the heavens, who took me from my father's home and the country of my relatives, who talked to me and swore to me, I will give this country to your descendants, will send His angel ahead of you, and you will get a wife there for my son. (Genesis 24:7 AAT)

Eliezer relayed this message to Laban and his family:

> "He answered me, 'The LORD, before whom I have lived, will send His angel with you. He will make your trip successful, and you will get my son a wife from my relatives, from my father's family.' " (Genesis 24:40 AAT)

Abraham assured Eliezer that the Mal'akh would be the One whom God would send to bring him safely and successfully through his journey in seeking a wife for Isaac. Here Abraham points to the Mal'akh as God's guide for the development of his fledgling nation. God himself speaks of the Mal'akh this way, as we noted previously in Exodus 23:20-23. The Lord declares that the Mal'akh will guide his people to the Promised Land. Moses speaks of the Mal'akh in this sense when he says:

> "We cried to the LORD, and He heard us and sent an angel who took us out of Egypt." (Numbers 20:16 AAT)

The picture is always the same, God sends his Angel to preserve, protect, guide and bless his people.

Well might Jacob have prayed to the Mal'akh in the afore mentioned manner, for if we turn back to his younger years, we find the Mal'akh constantly saving him from harm. We recall the wondrous dream which Jacob had at Bethel when he fled from death at the hands of his brother, Esau. He saw a ladder stretching from earth to heaven, on which the created angels of God were descending and ascending. This ladder extended from the earth at Bethel to the presence of God who stood above it and said to him, "I am Jehovah, the God of your father Abraham and the God of Isaac." He promised to be with Jacob and to grant him peace and protection where he was going. He would also bring him safely back home. Little wonder that Jacob exclaimed on awaking:

"How awesome is this place!" (Genesis 28:17 NIV)

Jacob called the place Bethel which means the "House of God." He vowed that as long as he lived he would serve the God who had appeared to him, if God would bring him safely back home some day. This passage alone might not seem to have any relation to the Mal'akh, but if we turn to Genesis 31 we will see that evil was again upon Jacob and that the Mal'akh appeared to him saying, "I am the God of Bethel." Here the Mal'akh tells Jacob that he is the God Jacob had seen at Bethel, that he had blessed Jacob and that it was now time to return home. He promised Jacob that he would be with him and reminded him of the vow Jacob had made at Bethel years before.

Nowhere in Scripture are vows made to mere angels. And when vows were made to God, they were considered binding, requiring literal fulfillment — anything less being a sin. In Genesis 31:13 we noted that the Mal'akh claims that Jacob's vow had been made to him, the vow of lifelong service and worship. He demanded its fulfillment.

In faith Jacob returned home. As he came near, Jacob began to worry about what his brother Esau might do to him. After all, he had left home in the first place because Esau was ready to kill him. Worried and perplexed Jacob took a walk in the night. Suddenly he met a man who forced him to fight. Scripture says of this:

> And Jacob was left alone, and a Man wrestled with him until the ascending of the dawn. And He saw that He had not prevailed against Him; and He struck the hollow of his thigh; and the hollow of Jacob's thigh was out of joint as he wrestled with Him. And He said, Send me away, for the dawn has ascended. And he said, I will not let You go unless You bless me. And He said to him, What is your name? And he said, Jacob. And He said, Your name shall no longer be called Jacob, but Israel; because you have wrestled with God and with men and have prevailed. And Jacob asked and said, Please reveal Your name. And He said, Why then do you ask about My name? And He blessed him there. And Jacob called the name of the place Penuel, because I saw God face to face, and my life is preserved. (Genesis 32:24-30 Gr.)

Through the late hours of the night the fight continued and Jacob came to realize who his antagonist was. When dawn began to break the opponent crippled Jacob by miraculously shrinking a muscle in his leg. Even though crippled, Jacob clung to his adversary. Jacob refused to let him go until he was blessed. Having refused to quit without being granted a blessing, Jacob received a rich blessing, a new name. No more was he to be called Jacob, — which means "the Supplanter," "the Cheater" — but Israel, "the Prince of God," or "Warrior of God." He knew he had wrestled with God and seen him face to face. Therefore he named the place Peniel ("face of God"), and exclaimed:

> I have seen God face to face, and my life is preserved. (Genesis 32:30 KJV)

The prophet Hosea sheds considerable light on this passage when he refers back to Jacob and says:

> He took his brother by the heel in the womb, and by his strength he contended with God. Yes, he wept and pleaded to Him, and he contended with the Angel and overcame. He finds us at Bethel, and there He speaks with us, even Jehovah the God of hosts. Jehovah is his memorial. (Hosea 12:3-5 Gr.)

Hosea here refers to Jacob's wrestling with the man. He refers to this man as Mal'akh and also calls him the God of Bethel and the Lord of hosts. Little wonder that Jacob on his deathbed prayed over his grandsons as we noted in Genesis 48:16, "The Angel which redeemed me from all evil bless the lads." Jacob knew the Angel as a distinct person of God himself. He knew and loved him as his Redeemer from all evil.

The Mal'akh as Divine Deliverer

Four centuries later a man named Moses was herding sheep on Mount Horeb when suddenly his attention was drawn to the sight of a bush burning. Strangely enough, the bush did not burn up even though the fire raged within it. This phenomenon aroused his curiosity and he decided to go over to the bush and discover the reason for such an unnatural occurrence. As Moses drew near, he was suddenly addressed by the Mal'akh Jahweh, who told him to remove his shoes for the ground on which he stood was holy ground, sanctified by the presence of the Mal'akh. Moses then heard the awesome introduction of the Being he confronted, in the words, "I am the God of Abraham, the God of Isaac, and the God of Jacob." Moses, in speechless terror, hid his face because he was afraid to look on God. He recognized the Mal'akh as God, and yet the Mal'akh is pictured as being other than God in person.

In this portion of Scripture (Exodus 3) the terms Elohim and Jahweh are used interchangeably with the term Mal'akh. Not only did the Mal'akh call himself God (Exodus 3:6), but he told Moses that he was the "I Am" God. In other words, he is the only and sole-existent God in the universe. He declared that he was the God of Moses' fathers, saying:

> And God said to Moses, I AM THAT I AM; and He said, You shall say this to the children of Israel, I AM has sent me to you. And God said to Moses again, You shall say this to the children of Israel, Jehovah the God of your fathers, the God of Abraham, the God of Isaac, and the God of Jacob, has sent me to you; this is My name forever, and this is My title from generation to generation. (Exodus 3:14,15 Gr.)

Furthermore, the Angel commanded Moses to go and deliver the Israelites because their prayers had come to him. Moses kept whining and making excuses until the Mal'akh became angry. He rebuked Moses sharply and claimed to be the Creator of man and hence the final authority on what a man is and is not capable of doing:

> And Jehovah said to him, Who has made man to speak? Or who makes the dumb, or the deaf, or the seeing, or the blind? Is it not I, Jehovah? (Exodus 4:11 Gr.)

He also commanded Moses to perform miracles in his name. Needless to say, Moses went to Egypt and boldly declared before Pharaoh:

> Thus says Jehovah the God of Israel, Send away My people, that they may hold a feast to Me in the wilderness. (Exodus 5:1 Gr.)

Pharaoh was to know that the Lord God of Israel demanded the release of his people Israel.

Moses courageously and faithfully carried out God's commands. God judged Egypt through the ten plagues; he also rendered Egypt powerless to attempt any reprisals against the children of Israel for years to come by systematically destroying it through the removal of its food supply, its stability, its wealth and its army. The Angel of the Lord led his people through the Red Sea toward Mt. Sinai in a pillar of cloud by day and a pillar of fire by night.

For the next forty years the visible presence of the Mal'akh was with Israel by day and night in the cloud. Scripture says of this:

> Behold, I am about to send an Angel before you, to guard you in the way, and to bring you to the place which I have prepared. Be careful before Him, and listen to His voice;

do not be rebellious against Him; for He will not forgive your transgressions, for My name is in Him. For if you completely listen to His voice, and do all which I speak, I will be an enemy to your enemies, and will be an adversary to your adversaries. For My Angel shall go before you and bring you in to the Amorites, and the Hittites, and the Perizzites, and the Canaanites, the Hivites, and the Jebusites; and I will destroy them.

You shall not bow yourself to their gods, and you shall not serve them, and you shall not do according to their works; but you shall surely tear them down, and you shall surely break their idols into pieces. And you shall serve Jehovah your God, and He will bless your bread and your water; and I will remove sickness from your midst. (Exodus 23:20-25 Gr.)

God here told his people that he was sending the Angel before them as their Guide. In this way God showed the Mal'akh to be a separate person in the Godhead. He also demonstrated the divine stature of the Mal'akh by pointing out that the Mal'akh has as a part of his being the name of God and that he wields the power to forgive sins. No mere angel has the name of God as a part of his being and no angel has the authority to forgive sins. Only God possesses this authority.

In Exodus 33 God further describes the divine nature of the Mal'akh:

Moses said to the LORD, "You have been telling me, 'Lead these people,' but you have not let me know whom you will send with me. You have said, 'I know you by name and you have found favor with me.' If I have found favor in your eyes, teach me your ways so I may know you and continue to find favor with you. Remember that this nation is your people." The Lord replied, "My Presence will go with you, and I will give you rest." Then Moses said to him, "If your Presence does not go with us, do not send us up from here. How will anyone know that you are pleased with me and with your people unless you go with us? What else will distinguish me and your people from all the other people on the face of the earth?" And the Lord said to Moses, "I will do the very thing you have asked, because I am pleased with you and I know you by name." (Exodus 33:12-17 NIV)

In these words God is answering Moses' prayer for divine guidance on the journey which lay ahead. God says, "my face" or "presence" will go with you. The "face" of Jehovah is God's own personal presence. It is identical with the "Angel" who was to lead Israel and in whom the name of Jehovah was. Jesus' words are also very interesting in this respect:

"Anyone who has seen me has seen the Father." (John 14:9 NIV)

That the Mal'akh who led Israel was Christ and that he wielded the divine power of judgment, St. Paul underscores when he writes:

Nor would we try Christ, as also some of them tested Him and were slain by serpents. (1 Corinthians 10:9 KJ II)

In the book of Numbers Moses refers to the Mal'akh and how he led the Israelites:

"We cried to the LORD, and He heard us and sent an angel who took us out of Egypt. Now we're here in Kadesh, a town on the edge of your territory." (Numbers 20:16 AAT)

Moses had sent emissaries to Edom, asking permission to pass through the country. He said that the prayers of the Israelites during the period of slavery in Egypt resulted in God sending the Mal'akh who had brought them out of Egypt and led them to the borders of Edom.

As we briefly noted earlier, when Israel had entered Canaan and laid siege to Jericho the Mal'akh appeared to Joshua, who had succeeded Moses as the civil leader of Israel. There we saw the Mal'akh's divine power. Here let us note his divine majesty:

> And it came to pass, when Joshua was beside Jericho, that he lifted up his eyes and looked, and, behold, a Man stood opposite him, and His drawn sword was in His hand; and Joshua went to Him, and said to Him, Are You for us, or for our foes? And He said, No, for I now come as the Captain of the army of Jehovah! And Joshua fell on his face to the earth, and worshiped, and said to Him, What does my Lord say to His servant? And the Captain of the army of Jehovah said to Joshua, Take your shoe off your foot, for the place on which you are standing is holy; and Joshua did so. (Joshua 5:13-15 Gr.)

Joshua had gone for a walk in the evening to think about the problems confronting him, when suddenly the Mal'akh as an armed warrior stood before him with drawn sword. Joshua approached him and challenged him demanding identification. The warrior replied that he had come to Joshua as the Captain of the hosts of God, or the Prince of the army of Jahweh. Joshua fell on his face and worshiped the Messenger of God, thus acknowledging him as God. The Prince of God accepted this worship and told Joshua to take off his shoes for the ground about him was sanctified by his presence. It is interesting to note that in both the appearances to Moses and Joshua, the removal of the shoes is repeated, only in this case the Mal'akh calls himself the Prince of God. Scripture here calls the Prince or Captain, Jahweh or Jehovah:

> And Jehovah said to Joshua, See, I have given Jericho and its king, mighty warriors, into your hand. (Joshua 6:2 Gr.)

While the incident designates the Mal'akh as God, it again shows him to be a separate person within the Godhead.

As the years passed in the Promised Land, Israel fell from the Lord and became idolatrous. God at such times delivered his people into the hands of their enemies. When the Israelites repented, God raised up a person who would deliver them. Gideon was one such man.

We have already discussed Judges 6:11-24, where the Mal'akh appeared to Gideon and told him to go and deliver his people from the Midianites. Gideon wanted to be sure of the fact that God was actually appointing him to the task. For this reason he asked the Mal'akh to receive an offering at his hands. The Mal'akh said he would wait for him to bring the offering. Scripture explicitly relates that it was the Mal'akh who appeared and that it was the Mal'akh who instructed Gideon to go and deliver Israel. Gideon was to go, having been sent by the Mal'akh and upheld by the Mal'akh's might.

When Gideon brought an offering, the Mal'akh told him to place it on a rock. He then touched it with his staff and a miraculous fire rose out of the rock and consumed the offering. After this sacrifice, the Angel vanished, leaving Gideon terrified and in fear of death. Scripture says Gideon knew that his visitor had been the Mal'akh Jahweh, and that he had seen him face to face. As a result Gideon was filled with fear:

> And Gideon saw that He was the Angel of Jehovah; and Gideon said, Alas, Lord Jehovah! Because I have seen the Angel of Jehovah face to face! (Judges 6:22 Gr.)

Then Scripture states that Jahweh, not the Mal'akh, assured Gideon that he would not die:

> And Jehovah said to him, Peace to you, fear not, you shall not die. (Judges 6:23 Gr.)

Again the name of God is applied to the Mal'akh. It also should be noted that the fear of death was often inspired by the appearance of the Mal'akh to men.

After the Israelites had been delivered from the Midianites according to the word of the Angel, they again became unfaithful and were afflicted by the Philistines. We previously cited Judges 13, in which two appearances of the Mal'akh Jahweh are recorded, one to the wife of Manoah, and one to both Manoah and his wife. The purpose of the appearances was to announce the birth of a deliverer, a man who would fight in divinely given strength, the Nazarite Samson. When Manoah prayed for a second visitation, it was granted. And when Manoah asked permission to prepare a lamb for him, the

Mal'akh said he would not eat of it but that as a burnt offering it would be acceptable to God. Manoah then asked for the Mal'akh's name and was told:

> Why do you ask My name, seeing it is Wonderful? (Judges 13:18 Ber.)

(It is interesting to compare this self-naming with the naming of the Messiah as "Wonderful" in Isaiah 9:6.)

As soon as the offering was ready it was presented to the Mal'akh who caused it to be consumed in miraculous fire. He vanished in the flame and did not reappear. Manoah and his wife then realized that their visitor had been none other than the Mal'akh Jahweh. The terror of death rested on Manoah and he exclaimed:

> "We shall surely die because we have looked upon God." (Judges 13:22 Ber.)

In this section, it is the Mal'akh that appears. He accepts a sacrifice as God. He is recognized as God. He is termed both Elohim and Jahweh, the names for God.

Because of all he had done, the Old Testament people of God knew of the Mal'akh. And because of all he had done for them, they loved, feared and revered him. This is brought out clearly in the second book of Samuel:

> "So your maidservant has requested, 'Please, may the decision of my master the king be one that sets the situation at ease; because as the Angel of God, so is my master the king, to discern right and wrong.' The Lord your God be with you." (2 Samuel 14:17 Ber.)
>
> "It was to place the matter in a different light that your servant Joab did this thing, but my master has percep-

tion like the wisdom of the Angel of God, so as to know everything on the earth!" (2 Samuel 14:20 Ber.)

David had to be asked to allow his son Absalom to return from exile by Joab. This request was made through a wise woman of Tekoa. David saw Joab's influence behind all this and inquired whether Joab had asked her to make the request. The woman responded by comparing David's wisdom to that of the Mal'akh who was all wise and knew everything that went on in the land. No mere angel has such wisdom, only God does. The Mal'akh is credited here with the wisdom of God. He was looked on as divine.

The divine honor and glory accorded the Mal'akh by the Old Testament is again shown vividly in the book of Zechariah. Here the Messianic time is spoken of as being a time of great glory. It was to be the time in which the house of David would reach its greatest moment. The glory of the house of David would be as Elohim or God, as the Mal'akh Jahweh:

> "On that day the LORD will shield those who live in Jerusalem, so that the feeblest among them will be like David, and the house of David will be like God, like the Angel of the LORD going before them." (Zechariah 12:8 NIV)

The Mal'akh as Messiah

Finally, approximately four hundred years before Christ, Malachi refers to the Mal'akh saying:

> "*I am going to send My messenger to prepare a way for Me.* And the LORD whom you're looking for will suddenly come to His temple, yes, the Angel of the covenant whom you delight in — He will come," says the LORD of armies. But when He comes, *who can bear it?* When He shows Himself, *who can stand it?* He is like a refiner's fire, like cleaners' soap. And He will sit down like one who refines and cleanses silver to cleanse Levi's descendants and purify them like gold and silver. Then they will in a righteous way bring offerings to the LORD. (Malachi 3:1-3 AAT)

The Mal'akh who had played such a tremendous role in the history of the Jews, who had helped them again and again, who had become to them a source of delight — he it was who would appear as the One sent by God for the sake of men. When he came, his mission would be to cleanse, to purify, and to judge. Malachi thus pictures the Messianic mission of the Mal'akh to be the climactic one. He would appear once more to redeem and cleanse Israel from all evil through judgment. This redemptive and yet punitive mission of the Mal'akh is in perfect harmony with his many appearances in the Old Testament. Isaiah also speaks of such a visitation by the Mal'akh or Messiah, saying:

> Who is this coming from Edom, from Bozrah, with his garments stained crimson? Who is this, robed in splendor,

striding forward in the greatness of his strength? "It is I, speaking in righteousness, mighty to save." Why are your garments red, like those of one treading the winepress? "I have trodden the winepress alone; from the nations no one was with me. I trampled them in my anger and trod them down in my wrath; their blood spattered my garments, and I stained all my clothing. For the day of vengeance was in my heart, and the year of my redemption has come. I looked, but there was no one to help, I was appalled that no one gave support; so my own arm worked salvation for me, and my own wrath sustained me. I trampled the nations in my anger; in my wrath I made them drunk and poured their blood on the ground."

I will tell of the kindnesses of the LORD, the deeds for which he is to be praised, according to all the LORD has done for us — yes, the many good things he has done for the house of Israel, according to his compassion and many kindnesses. He said, "Surely they are my people, sons who will not be false to me"; and so he became their Savior. In all their distress he too was distressed, and the angel of his presence saved them. In his love and mercy he redeemed them; he lifted them up and carried them all the days of old. (Isaiah 63:1-9 NIV)

Elsewhere in the book of Isaiah God declares:

I am the LORD: that is my name: and my glory will I not give to another, neither my praise to graven images. (Isaiah 42:8 KJV)

Such worship, praise and honor the Mal'akh always received. Certainly he was not Satan acting as God's messenger. Nor was he a mere angel, for any angel would have sinned by doing and claiming all the Mal'akh did. He was a separate person within the Godhead, true God himself.

In the mind of the writer, the Mal'akh's victorious role of delivering Israel from slavery and leading it to the glory of the Promised Land was one of the basic reasons for the delusions which the people of Jesus' time had concerning the mission of the Messiah. Since, as mentioned above, Malachi 3:1-3 speaks of the Mal'akh as the coming Messiah, one can understand the Jews' perversion of the truth. They knew from the Old Testament that the principal task of the Mal'akh had been the founding, guiding and protecting of the chosen race. He had led them into the Promised Land and had driven out all their enemies before them, until the Israelites resorted to idolatry. After the terrible Babylonian captivity the people were determined never to repeat the mistake of committing idolatry. And in not repeating it, in hewing to the letter of the law, they looked forward to another glorious manifestation of the Mal'akh. They expected he would again lead them against all physical foes and reestablish them in the Promised Land, giving them back the kingdom of David. Thus they felt that the purging, refining and judgment of his promised coming would not be directed against his chosen people, but against their enemies.

The Jews of Jesus' day were willing to acknowledge the Messiah as the Mal'akh of God, willing to acknowledge his power over history and nations, but unwilling to accept his judgment of them because of their sins and their need for repentance. Neither were they willing to accept the Messiah as the Ebed Jahweh, that is, the suffering Savior from sin. The Mal'akh had never suffered, but had always been victorious. They would not believe the suffering and death of the Mal'akh as the way to victory over sin. They would not believe in spite of the sacrifices with which they worshiped and the prophecies, beginning with Genesis 3:15, which portrayed the suffering death of the Savior as the necessary prelude to his eternal reign with his redeemed in glory.

The Mal'akh Called God
and Christ in the New Testament

The concept of the Mal'akh was not an unknown thing to the New Testament believers. Instead, it served as a source of witness to the many gracious dealings of God with his people in Old Testament times.

We read in the book of Acts:

> "And so forty years passed. Then *an Angel appeared to him in the wilderness* of Mount Sinai *in the flames of a burning thornbush.* Moses was surprised to see this. As *he went closer to examine it, the Lord said, 'I am the God of your fathers, the God of Abraham, Isaac, and Jacob.'* Moses started to tremble and *didn't dare to look. The Lord told him, 'Take your shoes off; the place where you're standing is holy ground. I have seen how my people are mistreated in Egypt, I have heard their groaning and have come down to rescue them. And now come, I will send you to Egypt.'*
>
> "This Moses whom they rejected by saying, '*Who made you ruler and judge?*' this one God sent to rule and free them with the help of the Angel he saw in the thornbush. He led them out, doing *startling wonders and miracles in Egypt*, at the Red Sea, and *for forty years in the desert.* It was this Moses who told the Israelites: *God will raise one of your people to be a Prophet to you like me.* Moses was in the congregation in the wilderness with the Angel who

spoke to him on Mount Sinai and with our fathers. He received living truths to give you, but our fathers refused to obey him. Yes, they rejected him, and their hearts *turned away to Egypt.*" (Acts 7:30-39 AAT)

St. Stephen here refers to the call of Moses by God at the burning bush which we discussed earlier. He says that Moses was sent by the hand of the Angel or Mal'akh, who appeared to him in the bush. When he quotes the conversation he says God spoke to Moses, finally stating that the Angel sent Moses to deliver Israel. Stephen, too, equates the Mal'akh and God. Stephen even goes so far as to state that Moses spoke with the Mal'akh at Mt. Sinai. This would certainly mean that he considered the Mal'akh to be God.

St. Paul also refers to the Mal'akh when he says:

> For I do not want you to be ignorant of the fact, brothers, that our forefathers were all under the cloud and that they all passed through the sea. They were all baptized into Moses in the cloud and in the sea. They all ate the same spiritual food and drank the same spiritual drink; for they drank from the spiritual rock that accompanied them, and that rock was Christ. Nevertheless, God was not pleased with most of them; their bodies were scattered over the desert. (1 Corinthians 10:1-5 NIV)

Here Paul speaks of the gracious guidance, protection and provision given the Israelites as they journeyed from Egypt to the Promised Land. He culminates the passage by stating that all the Israelites passed through the sea, and were all baptized there "into Moses." Furthermore, they were all under the cloud and were all baptized in it unto Moses. All Israel also drank the same spiritual drink, for they all ate and drank through the bounty of the Rock that accompanied them. Paul undoubtedly is referring to Moses' song in Deuteronomy where God is spoken of as the Rock of Israel, who had so marvelously sustained them:

"The Rock! *What* He *does* is *perfect*, yes, all His ways *are right.*"

"You forget the Rock who bore you and no longer think of the God who gave you birth."

"How else could one chase a thousand or two make ten thousand flee if their Rock hadn't sold them and the LORD hadn't given them up? Our Rock isn't like their rock — our enemies testify to this." (Deuteronomy 32:4,18,30,31 AAT)

That the concept of God as the Rock of Israel is common in the Old Testament can readily be seen by such passages as:

"There is no one holy like the LORD; there's no one besides You, there is no rock like our God." (1 Samuel 2:2 AAT)

Is there any God beside the LORD? Is there any Rock beside our God? (Psalm 18:31 AAT)

I'm calling You, O LORD, O my Rock, don't turn silently away from me. (Psalm 28:1 AAT)

Surely He is my Rock and my Savior, my mountain Refuge where I'll not be shaken. (Psalm 62:2 AAT)

But the LORD has been my mountain Refuge, and my God is a Rock that shelters me. (Psalm 94:22 AAT)

From such passages as these we can conclude that Paul was referring to God as following the Jews in their exodus. We have already studied Exodus 13:21; 14:19,24; 23:20-25; and Numbers 20:16; these are all passages with which Paul was certainly familiar. According to these portions of Scripture, the Mal'akh Jahweh led the children of Israel in the exodus. Paul says the Rock or God who followed the children of Israel in their journey was Christ. It can definitely be said, then, that the Mal-'akh and Christ were one and the same in the mind of Paul.

It could not be otherwise, for the Rock which Paul speaks of as Christ, followed the children of Israel through the Red Sea and went with them for forty years. It miraculously fed them and gave them drink when needed. It was a spiritual Rock, not physical. It moved about. As a divine Being it provided both the physical and spiritual needs of over two million people for forty years. It certainly was not some physical rock which rolled along after them and miraculously provided for them. No physical rock could do these things. The obvious meaning is that the Rock spoken of here was Christ, the Mal'akh Jahweh of the Old Testament, and was understood to be so by Paul, writing by inspiration.

In 1 Corinthians 10:9 Paul also refers to the Mal'akh and calls him Christ:

> Nor would we try Christ, as also some of them tested Him and were slain by serpents. (KJ II)

Here Paul is speaking of the plague of snakes which was sent on the rebellious Israelites toward the end of the forty years of wandering. The Mal'akh had led them for the entire time in the pillar of cloud and fire. Though God the Father had warned the Israelites not to sin against the

Mal'akh, they still tempted him and drew upon themselves the divine judgment of the Mal'akh. Paul says they tempted Christ when they did this. There he again refers to the Mal'akh as Christ, thus making the Mal'akh and Christ one and the same.

Having seen the tremendous role of the Mal'akh in developing and protecting the people of God in the Old Testament, is it any wonder that God personally named him Jesus before he was born into the world? Jesus means Savior. His role throughout the Old Testament had always been that of the Savior of God's people. What more fitting name could be given him in the New Testament than Jesus, Savior! In the New Testament he would continue that role and bring it to its climax by living and dying as the Savior of all mankind and the conqueror of sin, death and hell.

Summary of the Mal'akh Jahweh

Through the years many Bible critics have tried to belittle the majestic and divine stature of the Angel of the Lord. But all their arguments and protests are useless against this Rock, as Paul calls him. To endless ages he will be loved, worshiped and adored — Christ, our Rock of Ages, the Mal'akh Jahweh of the Old Testament. If we would try to draw up a list of scriptural truths concerning the Mal'akh, truths known to Jewish believers at the time of Jesus, the following would be representative:

1. The Mal'akh Jahweh is superior to created angels and serves as God's special Messenger, declaring and carrying out God's will.

2. He controls the destinies of nations for the welfare of his people.
3. He has power to forgive, to judge and to punish sins.
4. He has power over Satan, and Satan recognizes his power.
5. He accepts sacrifices and worship.
6. He is separate from God as to his person.
7. He is God.
8. He participated in the work of creation.
9. He is the promised Messiah.
10. He is Jesus Christ.

5. THE SERVANT OF THE LORD —
THE EBED JAHWEH

The Servant Poems of Isaiah

The full picture of the coming Messiah in the Old Testament is shown through a combination of roles portrayed in biblical history and prophecy. One epic role is that of the Ebed Jahweh, or the Servant of the Lord. This role is found mainly in four poems in the book of Isaiah, called by biblical scholars the Servant poems. They point with singular clarity to the Ebed Jahweh as the Servant of the Lord who was to bring God's salvation and truth to all people.

The role of the Messiah as the Servant of God, however, was not just a role spoken of in the Old Testament. It was also known to the New Testament believers. In the book of Acts, Peter refers to Christ as the Servant of God and says:

> "Now that God has given His Servant, He sent Him first
> to you to bless you by turning every one of you from your
> wicked ways." (Acts 3:26 AAT)

The Servant poems were loved, known and believed by God's people from the time that they were first written. In these poems the faithful saw their Messiah, for whom they longed and waited. There are four main songs; some add a fifth, Isaiah 61. We shall consider only the four main poems.

Christ as the
Servant of the Lord

God
the Father

Sin

Hill of Atonement

The first Servant poem could well be entitled "God's Missionary to the World":

> Behold My servant, whom I uphold, My elect in whom My soul delights! I have put My Spirit upon Him, He shall bring forth judgment to the nations; He shall not cry or shout aloud, or cause His voice to be heard in the street; a bruised reed He shall not break, and a dimly burning wick He shall not quench; but He shall bring forth justice in agreement with truth; He shall not fail nor- be suppressed, until He has established justice in the earth; the islands will await His teaching. Thus says the only God, the LORD, who created the heavens and stretched them out, who spread out the earth with all its vegetation; who gives breath to the people upon it and spirit to them who walk therein: I, the LORD, have called you in righteousness; I will hold your hand and guard you and give you as a covenant for the people, as a light for the Gentiles to open blind eyes, to bring captives out of prison, and those who sit in darkness out of houses of bondage. (Isaiah 42:1-7 Ber.)

Behold, God says, look at my servant, the one whom I place before you as my own chosen Ambassador. My soul delights in him. He is no ordinary servant. He bears within him the Spirit of God. His is a gigantic task, to place the truths of God before the gentiles of the world. He will not be a boisterous servant; he will not seek public acclaim. The penitent and sorrowing sinner he will not despise or condemn, and the man of weak faith he will not destroy. He will present to them the gracious truths of God in faithfulness and love. Nothing will be able to turn him aside from his appointed task. He will not cease working till the truths of God have covered the earth, reaching even the remotest isle.

The majesty of this poem is ever enhanced by the progress of the gospel in the world today. The Ebed Jahweh was not only to be placed before the Jews, but also before the gentiles. As he carried out his God-given task of confronting the world with the truth of God, there resided in him the Spirit of God. He thus would become the comfort of the sorrowing, the strength of the weak, the inspiration of the strong. His mission would be an ongoing one that nothing could turn aside. He himself would see that the Word of God would reach the remotest isle.

The second Servant poem could well be called "The Redemption of the World":

> Listen to me, you islands, and pay attention, you peoples from afar! The LORD called me from my birth, from the body of my mother He has caused my name to be remembered. He made my mouth like a sharp sword and in the shadow of His hand He hid me; He made me a polished arrow, and in His quiver He concealed me. He said to me, You are My Servant, Israel, in whom I will be glorified. But I said, "I have labored in vain, I have spent my strength for nothing; nevertheless surely my right is at the LORD's disposal and my recompense rests with God." But now the LORD, who formed me from my birth to be His Servant, to bring Jacob back to Him and that Israel might be gathered for Him — for I am honorable in the LORD's eyes and my God is my strength — He says: It is too light a thing that you should be My Servant, to raise up the tribes of Jacob and to restore the preserved of Israel; I will make you a light to the nations that My salvation may reach to the end of the earth. (Isaiah 49:1-6 Ber.)

The Servant of the Lord addresses the remotest isles and calls on the most distant nations to listen to his song.

174

They should listen while he instructs them about himself and his mission. He says that God has called him from the womb and that from the time his mother first carried him in the womb God had named him. God fashioned and protected him for a specific task. He made his mouth like a sharp sword. He was kept safely in the quiver of God as the Lord's choicest arrow until the time was come for him to be launched on his mission. Then, when the time came, God sent him saying he was the chosen Servant of God. He was to live for Israel, in its stead before God, that God in him might be glorified. The work was long and hard, and it seemed he was alone, forsaken and despised. Yet he rested his case before the Lord and trusted God to vindicate him. This God did, and sent him to bring back Jacob and gather Israel.

Because his Servant had done the difficult work assigned to him, God glorified him. The Lord showed that he was not only the Servant of God to the tribes of Jacob, but also a light for all the gentiles, a beacon of salvation to the ends of the earth.

The Servant is presented as a specially designed instrument of God. He was to be a man, named by God before birth. His mission was to teach men about God and for this reason he was gifted with a sword-like mouth. He would faithfully carry out God's mission of salvation, being the substitute for Israel before God, and in him God would be glorified. He would be humbled but exalted above all, for he would be made the Light of salvation for the whole world. Perhaps it was of this song that Simeon thought when he said:

For mine eyes have seen thy salvation, ... a light to lighten the Gentiles, and the glory of thy people Israel. (Luke 2:30-32 KJV)

The third Servant poem could be named "Mission of Victory":

The Lord God has given me a tongue to know how to speak a timely word to the weary. He awakens every morning, He alerts my ear to hear as a student. The Lord God has opened my ear, I have not been rebellious, I did not pull back. I gave my back to the smiters, my cheeks to those who plucked off my beard; I did not shield my face from insult and spitting. The Lord God is my helper; therefore I am not confounded, for I set my face like a flint; I know that I shall not be put to shame. He who vindicates me is near by. Who will contend with me? Let us take our stand together. Who is my adversary? Let him come near to me. Behold, the Lord God helps me; who is he that can condemn me? Take note, all of them will wear out like a garment; moth will consume them! (Isaiah 50:4-9 Ber.)

In this poem the Servant further illustrates his mission among men by saying that God has given him the ability to speak eloquently so he would be able to cheer the weary and heartsick when they needed it. He would do nothing of himself. Rather, he would walk before God as a disciple, carrying out God's instructions day by day. We see the fulfillment of this in Christ:

Then Jesus replied to them, "I truly assure you that, the Son is not able to do anything by Himself, but only what He sees the Father doing; whatever He does, the Son does in the same way . . . . I can do nothing independently; I judge as I am informed and My judgment is fair; for I am

not looking out for My will but for the will of Him who
sent me." (John 5:19,30 Ber.)

So obedient would the Servant be that he would not
shun the climax of his mission even though it entailed
suffering. He would freely offer his back to the floggers
and his cheeks to those who wanted to pull out handfuls
of beard. He would not hide his face when they wanted to
shame him and spit in it. In all his suffering he would
remain confident of one thing, that God would be with
him and help him. In this hope he would face whatever lay
ahead; he would set his face like flint, knowing this was
not shame for him. In confidence and boldness he could
declare that God who would vindicate him was very near.
Secure in this confidence, the Servant would challenge all
in earth or hell to confront him in conflict. Who would
dare to confront him? God would help him — who, then,
would presume to condemn him? Whoever did would fall
to pieces like a moth-eaten garment.

"In all this I will remain confident," the Servant is
almost heard to say, "for God has given me the ability to
speak to people in need. God who has instructed me day
by day and who has helped me in my suffering will surely
vindicate me before all men. Who will dare to oppose me
when God has glorified me? Destruction awaits any that
do, for I am God's Servant."

The fourth Servant poem would best be titled, "The
Suffering and Exalted Servant":

> Behold, My Servant shall rule wisely, He shall be exalted
> and extolled and be very high. Just as many were aston-
> ished at You (His face was marred more than any man,

177

and His form more than the sons of men), so shall He sprinkle many nations. Concerning Him, kings shall shut their mouths; for that which was never told, they shall see; they shall understand that which they never heard. Who has believed our report? And to whom is the arm of the LORD revealed? For He shall grow up before Him as a tender plant, and as a root out of a dry ground. He has no form nor comeliness; and when we shall see Him, there is no beauty that we should desire Him. He is despised and rejected of men; a man of sorrows and acquainted with grief. And as it were, we hid our faces from Him; He is despised, and we esteemed Him not. Surely He has borne our griefs and carried our sorrows; yet we esteemed Him stricken, smitten of God and afflicted. But He was wounded for our transgressions; He was bruised for our iniquities; the chastisement of our peace was upon Him; and with His stripes we are healed. All we like sheep have gone astray; we have turned, each one, to his own way; and the LORD has laid on Him the iniquity of us all. He was oppressed, and He was afflicted; yet He opened not His mouth. He is brought as a lamb to the slaughter; and as a sheep before its shearers is dumb, so He opened not His mouth. He was taken from prison and from judgment; and who shall declare His generation? For He was cut off out of the land of the living; for the transgression of My people He was stricken. And He made His grave with the wicked, and with the rich in His death; because He had done no violence, and there was no deceit in His mouth. Yet it pleased the LORD to bruise Him. He has put Him to grief. When You shall make His soul an offering for sin, He shall see His seed. He shall prolong His days, and the LORD's will shall prosper in His hand. He shall see the fruit of the travail of His soul and shall be fully satisfied. By His knowledge shall My righteous Servant justify many, for He shall bear their iniquities. Therefore I will divide Him a portion with the great, and He shall divide the spoil with the strong; because He has poured out His soul to death; and He was counted among the transgressors; and He bore the sin of many and made intercession for the transgressors. (Isaiah 52:13-53:12 KJ II)

God presents his Servant to the world by saying that he would be exalted. The Lord then relates how this will take place. Many would see the Servant in his suffering and would be aghast at his appearance. His face and body would be inhumanly marred. In this way, however, he would cause many nations to exult in him. Kings would become silent when confronted with him for in him they will see what was not told them and in him they would be forced to consider what they had not heard.

Some say that the kings now try to justify their behavior by Isaiah 53; others say the prophet speaks on behalf of all people. Be that as it may, the universal cry goes out, "Who could have believed what we have heard?" To whom has the might of God been revealed? In other words, "What man could understand this or see God's might in it?"

The Servant will grow up before God as a sapling out of a dry ground. His family would have no status that would give him a reception before men. He would have no particular attraction in his person and when people would look on him there would be no particular beauty that they would desire him. In fact, he would be despised and forsaken by men, a man of sufferings and familiar with grief and disease, so that we and all men would pass him off lightly. This was reflected when Christ stood before Pilate:

But they cried out, Away! Away! Crucify him! Pilate said to them, Shall I crucify your king? The chief priests answered, We have no king except Caesar. (John 19:15 KJ II)

As we look at him now and consider him, we are compelled to say that he was carrying upon himself our sicknesses and griefs. He was carrying our pains and sorrows. When Christ suffered, it appeared that God was punishing him for his own sins. But in reality he was pierced for our sins. He was crushed for our evils. The punishment necessary for our peace was upon him and with his lash marks we are restored.

We must then admit that all of us have strayed like sheep, each of us has chosen his own particular path. Yet God in love has placed upon him the sin of us all. God's Servant was treated harshly. He was even tortured, but he never complained. Mocking, torturing and killing him was just like leading a lamb to the butcher, or like having a ewe sheared. He never objected. He was killed by oppression and judgment and who took to heart his fate?

He died with evildoers, but was buried as one of the rich, because he himself had done no sinful act, neither was any falsehood in his mouth. God saw fit to crush him and to punish him severely. The Lord made his Servant to be the offering for all sin, seemingly so guilty with sin, that men would say he deserved to die.

Yet by becoming this offering for man the Servant would be glorified. He himself would spread abroad his work of atonement and bring about the will of God among men. The effecting of the gracious will of God in mankind would now be turned over to him because of what he did for them. As this atonement would spread, he would see the results of his suffering in men and would be well satisfied. By the very evil done to him the Servant of God would make many righteous, for their sins would be transferred to him.

The Apostle John points to this truth when he says:

> My little children, I write these things to you so that you may not sin. And if anyone should sin, we have an Advocate with the Father, Jesus Christ the righteous; and He is the propitiation for our sins, but not for ours only, but also for all the world. (1 John 2:1,2 KJ II)

God says through Isaiah that he would grant his Servant greatness, and that his Servant, as a conqueror, will divide the spoils of his conquest with his followers. He would be granted this right because he had given up his life for mankind, being designated as a sinner by God and men. He thus carried upon himself the sins of mankind for mankind. In doing this, he pleaded effectually for all sinners.

This poem is surely one of comfort, beauty and power for any Christian. It places before men the vicarious atonement of the Ebed Jahweh. It shows plainly that as our substitute, he would be put to death, so that in him we might have eternal life. In view of the following New Testament passages it is incomprehensible that some deny Isaiah's prophecy of the vicarious atonement was fulfilled in Christ.

> So that which was spoken through Isaiah the prophet might be fulfilled, saying, "He took upon Himself our

weaknesses and bore our sicknesses." (Matthew 8:17 KJ II)

And the Scripture which says "And He was numbered with the lawless" was fulfilled. (Mark 15:28 KJ II)

Although He had done so many miracles before them, they did not believe on Him, so that the word of Isaiah the prophet might be fulfilled which he said, "Lord, who believed our report — and the arm of the Lord, to whom was it revealed?" (John 12:37,38 KJ II)

And the passage of the Scripture which he was reading was this, "He was led as a sheep to slaughter and as a lamb dumb before his shearer, so He does not open His mouth. In His humiliation His judgment was taken away, and who shall declare His generation? For His life is taken from the earth." And the eunuch answering to Philip said, I beg of you, about whom does the prophet say this, about himself or about some other? And Philip opened his mouth. And beginning from this Scripture, he preached to him the gospel of Jesus. (Acts 8:32-35 KJ II)

For He made Him who knew no sin to be sin for us, so that we might become the righteousness of God in Him. (2 Corinthians 5:21 KJ II)

Christ has ransomed us from the curse of the Law inasmuch as He became a curse for us, for it is written, "Cursed is every one who hangs on a tree." (Galatians 3:13 Ber.)

And in view of the fact that it is appointed to men once to die, and after this the Judgment — so Christ, having been once offered to bear the sins of many, shall appear a second time without sin to those that look for Him, to salvation. (Hebrews 9:27,28 KJ II)

He Himself bore our sins in His own body on the tree, so that we, being dead to sins, might live to righteousness —by whose stripes you were healed. For you were as sheep going astray, but you are now returned to the

Shepherd and Bishop of your souls. (1 Peter 2:24,25 KJ II)

Because even Christ once for all suffered for sins, the Just for the unjust, so that He might bring us to God, being put to death in the flesh but made alive by the Spirit. In which also, going to the spirits in prison, He preached. (1 Peter 3:18,19 KJ II)

Summary of the Ebed Jahweh
in the Old Testament Poems

According to *The Pulpit Commentary* in its explanation of Isaiah 53, until about A.D. 1150, the time of Aben Ezra, even the Jews acknowledged that the Servant poems pointed to the Messiah. After that time, however, the Jews abandoned this interpretation. They began to see in the Servant poems either some historic person other than the Messiah or else the entire nation of Israel. The interpretation of the Servant as being collective Israel seems to be favored by modern biblical critics. There is ground for this interpretation in a passage such as Isaiah 41:8, which speaks of the nation of Israel as the servant of the Lord. Nevertheless, the Servant poems we have discussed do not lend themselves to such an understanding. The Servant of the Lord, the Ebed Jahweh, has the following things said of him in these passages:

1. He is the Lord's Anointed (Messiah), a separate person in the Godhead.
2. He is sacrificed by God for the sin of mankind.
3. He would live among men and would be despised and rejected.
4. False judgment would condemn him to death.
5. He would be put to death with evildoers.

6. After his death he would lie in a rich man's tomb (cave).
7. He would rise from the dead and be the light of the world (gentiles) and spread his message and followers over the entire earth.
8. He would be exalted by God to rule heaven and earth.
9. He would be the judge of all mankind.

This was *the* Ebed Jahweh of the Old Testament. The Servant is spoken of in a very personal way and is granted glory and power that belong to God alone. It cannot, therefore, refer to a nation or a prophet. To the believing Jews of the New Testament, like Simeon, the Servant of the Lord was none other than the Messiah, the Savior of Israel and of the entire world.

6. THE PERSONIFIED "WISDOM OF GOD"

Three Views of Wisdom

In 1 Corinthians, Paul utters a truth that is familiar to all Christians. It is the truth that all who believe in Jesus acknowledge him as the power and the wisdom of God incarnate:

> We preach a crucified Christ. The Jews stumble over Him, the Greeks think He's something foolish, but to those who are called, both Jews and Greeks, He is Christ, God's power and God's wisdom. (1 Corinthians 1:23,24 AAT)

If one stops to consider the development and fulfillment of the plan of redemption against the backdrop of sinful man's history, one has to acknowledge that Christ is indeed the power of God incarnate. One also has to acknowledge the fact that the plan of redemption could only have been conceived by God and carried out by God. It is only fitting that the Son of God who carried out this plan be called the wisdom of God incarnate. When St. Paul proclaims Christ as the wisdom of God incarnate, he is personifying wisdom. It is interesting to note that this personification of "Wisdom" began already in the Old Testament. In Hebrew the term for wisdom is "chokmah" and in Greek "sophia."

Since the time of the apostles three general interpreta-

Christ as the
Wisdom of God

tions have been proposed for the word "wisdom" as found in the book of Proverbs.

1. The first view is that when the term "wisdom" is used in a supernatural or divine sense it refers only to an attribute of the Triune God. This becomes a deliberately biased type of thinking when one is confronted with the plain words of the text. Though an attribute may be personified it is never a divine person. Neither does it claim other divine attributes or powers for itself. Yet as we shall see from a number of sections of Proverbs, "wisdom" does this very thing.

2. Another school of thought admits the personification of wisdom but denies divinity to it. Grammatically speaking, the feminine form is used in Hebrew for the word "wisdom." It must be pointed out, however, that there are no neuter forms in Hebrew and all nouns must therefore be either masculine or feminine. The feminine form usually refers to those things which are without life, abstract ideas, countries, towns, parts of the body and powers of nature. The things to which the feminine form is attached are not necessarily feminine. For example, the word "fathers" has a feminine plural ending. Thus when wisdom in Proverbs is referred to in the feminine form, it does not mean that wisdom is a woman. It merely is done this way because the noun wisdom is classified as feminine.

3. The third view of personified "wisdom" in Proverbs is that it refers to the second Person of the Trinity. This view has been taken by a large number of the church fathers such as Irenaeus, Tertullian, Cyprian, Athanasius,

Gregory of Nyssa, Basil, Gregory Nazianzen, Hilary, Eusebius, Epiphanius, Jerome and Augustine, as well as by Luther and later commentators such as Hengstenberg and Matthew Henry. This is the present view of a number of conservative Lutherans, including this writer. In keeping with this interpretation we shall capitalize Wisdom when it refers to Christ.

Wisdom in Proverbs

The purpose of this book is to ascertain the faith of the Jews at the time of Christ on the basis of the message of the Old Testament. It is not meant to be a review of later believers' faith or unbelievers' doubts. With this in mind we will turn to the book of Proverbs and let it speak for itself. Already in the first chapter of Proverbs we are confronted with personified Wisdom:

> Wisdom calls aloud in the street, she raises her voice in the public squares; at the head of the noisy streets she cries out, in the gateways of the city she makes her speech:
>
> "How long will you simple ones love your simple ways? How long will mockers delight in mockery and fools hate knowledge? If you had responded to my rebuke, I would have poured out my heart to you and made my thoughts known to you. But since you rejected me when I called and no one gave heed when I stretched out my hand, since you ignored all my advice and would not accept my rebuke, I in turn will laugh at your disaster; I will mock when calamity overtakes you — when calamity overtakes you like a storm, when disaster sweeps over you like a whirlwind, when distress and troubles overwhelm you.
>
> "Then they will call to me but I will not answer; they will look for me but will not find me. Since they hated knowl-

edge and did not choose to fear the LORD, since they would not accept my advice and spurned my rebuke, they will eat the fruit of their ways and be filled with the fruit of their schemes. For the waywardness of the simple will kill them, and the complacency of fools will destroy them." (Proverbs 1:20-32 NIV)

Wisdom cries in the streets, markets, gates and gathering places, seeking to instill in sinful and foolish men the knowledge and fear of God. To anyone who will listen to her, she guarantees peace, safety and quietness from fear. But men are so corrupt that they simply ignore her plea. Because of this willful unbelief she pronounces doom and destruction upon all who do not listen and fear God. The call to repentance, the promise and the judgment are final, and as such would indicate they come from God.

The above mentioned portion of Scripture becomes exceedingly interesting and clear in the light of the words of Luke:

"The wisdom of God therefore says, 'I will send them prophets and apostles, some of whom they will kill and persecute,' so that the blood of all the prophets that has been shed from the foundation of the world may be charged against this generation, from Abel's blood to that of Zechariah, who was murdered between the altar and the temple. Yes, I tell you, it will be charged against this generation. Alas for you, teachers of the Law, for you have taken away the key to knowledge; you yourselves have not entered, and you have prevented those who were entering." (Luke 11:49-52 Ber.)

Here Jesus speaks of an eternal decree uttered by Wisdom in the interest of man's salvation. Wisdom would send prophets and apostles but they would be persecuted and killed by rebellious man. Because of man's treatment of these heaven sent messengers, an accounting will be exacted, vengeance will be taken. The reason for such divine judgment is that in the denial of Wisdom's invitation by the leaders of the Jews, the common people were deprived of the key to knowledge of eternal life. Truly "Wisdom" had cried throughout the land. Wisdom had cried through men of the Old Testament, but to no avail. Jesus applied this title to himself when he cried out to the men of his day and when he sent the apostles into all the world. They called out in his name to all mankind, just as Christians continue to do.

Another interesting passage of the New Testament in which Jesus refers to the unbelief of the Jews and terms himself the Wisdom of the Old Testament is found in Matthew with a parallel passage in Luke:

> "To what can I compare this generation? They are like children sitting in the marketplaces and calling out to others: 'We played the flute for you, and you did not dance; we sang a dirge, and you did not mourn.' For John came neither eating nor drinking, and they say, 'He has a demon.' The Son of Man came eating and drinking, and they say, 'Here is a glutton and a drunkard, a friend of tax collectors and "sinners." ' But wisdom is proved right by her actions." (Matthew 11:16-19 NIV)

> "To what, then, can I compare the people of this generation? What are they like? They are like children sitting in the marketplace and calling out to each other: 'We played the flute for you, and you did not dance; we sang a dirge, and you did not cry.' For John the Baptist came neither eating bread nor drinking wine, and you say, 'He has a demon.' The Son of Man came eating and drinking, and

you say, 'Here is a glutton and a drunkard, a friend of tax collectors and "sinners." ' But wisdom is proved right by all her children." (Luke 7:31-35 NIV)

Jesus says that the Jews of his time could be compared to children playing in a marketplace. But not all want to play the game. As a result, when the music was supposed to inspire a joyous reaction there was none, and when it was meant to inspire a mournful reaction there was none. There was no interest whatsoever in the game.

Similarly, when John came preaching repentance, and lived as a Nazarite, the reaction was that he was a demoniac. When Jesus came as a friend of sinners and a partaker in social life, he was called a drunkard, a glutton and a consort of sinners. The last words of Jesus are a pronouncement of judgment: "Wisdom is proved right by all her children." (NIV) "Wisdom is shown to be right by all her children." (AAT) "So is Wisdom vindicated by all her children." (Ber.) Jesus was thus vindicated by the indifference of the Jews to his message, according to the prophecy of Wisdom in the Old Testament. We are told in Proverbs that Wisdom sought the redemption of man, and that when man rejected her message the resultant doom was man's own fault. Thus Wisdom was vindicated of her children; Jesus was vindicated of the Jews as the perfect embodiment of Wisdom. Whether the Jews believed or not they bore the name of God's chosen people Israel, God's children, Wisdom's children, the Messiah's children. The tragedy was that they were disobedient and rebellious children whose behavior bore out the truth of the Wisdom of God.

Again we read in Proverbs:

> Blessed is the man who finds wisdom, the man who gains understanding, for she is more profitable than silver and yields better returns than gold. She is more precious than rubies; nothing you desire can compare with her. Long life is in her right hand; in her left hand are riches and honor. Her ways are pleasant ways, and all her paths are peace. She is a tree of life to those who embrace her; those who lay hold of her will be blessed. By wisdom the LORD laid the earth's foundations, by understanding he set the heavens in place; by his knowledge the deeps were divided, and the clouds let drop the dew. (Proverbs 3:13-20 NIV)

This section begins with a solemn admonition to the Christian not to rebel against the chastening of God, but to find in it a guide to a better Christian life. It is an encouragement to find Wisdom. Wisdom is portrayed as the greatest treasure a man can seek in this life. To those who find her she gives long life, wealth, honor, peace and joy. To show how great this Wisdom is, the writer says that God created the world by Wisdom. This passage also personifies Wisdom and raises her above a mere ability or store of knowledge in man's head. Certainly mere wisdom cannot grant a long life to anyone, only God can.

Scripture says of this:

> For with you is the fountain of life; in your light we see light. (Psalm 36:9 NIV)

Wisdom cannot grant peace, joy and life to an individual, for these are distinctly and completely gifts of God. Yet in this Proverbs passage, Wisdom is granting them. It is personified.

The personification of Wisdom is continued in Proverbs:

> "Get wisdom, get understanding; do not forget my words or swerve from them. Do not forsake wisdom, and she will protect you; love her, and she will watch over you. Wisdom is supreme; therefore get wisdom. Though it cost all you have, get understanding. Esteem her, and she will exalt you; embrace her, and she will honor you. She will set a garland of grace on your head and present you with a crown of splendor." (Proverbs 4:5-9 NIV)

Here the writer is relating the instruction he received from his father. He was told to make the acquisition of Wisdom the goal and purpose of his life, for Wisdom is the principal thing of life. If a man finds her, she will love him and keep him. She will exalt the person who exalts her and will grant him honor. Not only will she grant him honor, but will crown her finder with a crown of glory. A man dare not let her go, for with her his steps will not falter in life, for she is his life. Wisdom is here made the central aim of life, which cannot be justified, unless Wisdom is God. Wisdom is granted the ability to keep or sustain a man who finds her, to exalt him, grant him honor and a crown of glory. These gifts again are only God's to grant as Scripture points out, saying:

> You [God] will guide me with Your advice and finally take me to glory. (Psalm 73:24 AAT)
> Be faithful to death, and I will give you the crown of life. (Revelation 2:10 KJ II)

Moreover, it is stated in Proverbs that Wisdom is a man's life. God alone deserves this honor. Certainly Wisdom is here made more than mere head knowledge. Wisdom is personified and granted abilities of God alone.

The clearest and most interesting passage on the personification of Wisdom in the Old Testament is found in Proverbs 8. Wisdom is speaking in this section and says:

> The LORD possessed Me in the beginning of His way, before His works of old. I was set up from everlasting, from the beginning, before the earth ever was. When there were no depths, I was brought forth; when there were no mountains filled with water. Before the mountains were settled, before the hills, I was brought forth; before He had made the earth, or the fields, or the highest part of the dust of the world. When He prepared the heavens, I was there; when He set a circle on the face of the deep; when He set the clouds above; when He made the fountains of the deep strong; when He gave to the sea its limit, that the waters should not pass His commandment; when He appointed the foundations of the earth; then I was beside Him as one brought up with Him; and I was daily His delight, rejoicing always before Him; rejoicing in the part of His earth where men live; and My delights were with the sons of men. Now therefore listen to Me, O children; for blessed are those who keep My ways. Hear instruction, and be wise, and do not refuse it. Blessed is the man who hears Me, watching daily at My gates, waiting at the posts of My doors. For whoever finds Me finds life, and he shall obtain favor from the LORD. But he who sins against Me wrongs his own soul; all who hate Me love death. (Proverbs 8:22-36 KJ II)

Wisdom here speaks of her beginning and says that God possessed her in eternity. Before the earth was created she existed. She was brought forth in eternity, before there was any earth, sky, sea or land. When God uttered his decree of creation, she was there, the delight of God, rejoicing in him. She took special delight in man. Because

194

of her pre-existence, because of her presence with God at creation, because of her interest in man, all men are encouraged to listen to her, for before her they are but children. Blessed is the man who keeps her ways and daily waits upon her. Whoever finds her, finds life and obtains favor with God. But whoever refuses to follow her ways and ignores her instruction, sins against her and thus wrongs his own soul. Such a man hates Wisdom and because of this hate, loves death.

When one considers the claims advanced by Wisdom, it is inconceivable that mere knowledge is meant. Surely a man's wisdom was not born in eternity, nor has man's knowledge been a source of rejoicing to God. Man's wisdom of itself could have no special interest in man, for the mind of man is its generator, neither can it consider men children, for it is the child of man. Man is not blessed by wisdom for keeping the ways of wisdom, nor will this attract the favor of God. If a man ignores man's wisdom he does not sin or love death because of it. Man's wisdom is foolishness before God, as Scripture declares:

> For the wisdom of this world is foolishness in God's sight. As it is written: "He catches the wise in their craftiness"; and again, "The Lord knows that the thoughts of the wise are futile." (1 Corinthians 3:19, 20 NIV)

The only possible explanation is to permit the Proverbs text to speak for itself. Wisdom is then personified. She is eternal, with God from eternity and yet separate in person from him. Wisdom rules the earth, loves man and seeks his eternal welfare before God by imparting herself to them. She is the hope of man, his source of joy, success and peace. In her, man finds favor with God and life from him. Whoever spurns her, sins and draws death upon himself, because the absence of Wisdom in man is death. Described in this way, Wisdom is definitely personified and clearly pictured as a person of the Godhead.

To the writer, it is very clear that Wisdom in the Old Testament does in some cases refer to a divine Being, other than God in person, yet united with him; a Being possessed with all power, holiness, omniscience, grace, justice and kindness. In the passages we have considered Wisdom can be considered as a person in the Trinity, a separate person within the Godhead. As stated before, St. Paul unmistakably identified this Wisdom when he wrote:

> Christ, to them which are called, . . . [is] the wisdom of God. (1 Corinthians 1:24 KJV)

7. THE PERSONIFIED "WORD OF GOD"

The Old Testament and the Word

In the New Testament, the Apostle John uses the Greek term "Logos," "Word," as a proper name for Jesus. The author of this book believes that the root of the New Testament teaching of Jesus being the incarnate Word is to be found in the Old Testament concept of the personified Word, not in Greek philosophy or among the New Testament Gnostics as many advocate. John was steeped in the Old Testament as were all Jews, not in Greek thought. The Holy Spirit who inspired John certainly did not need pagan Greek thinking to present through John the concept of the Word as the Messenger of God. The Old Testament already says that God spoke through the Word. John identifies the Word as Christ. He does this to show that Jesus has from the beginning been the "Messenger," the "Mal'akh," the "Revealer" of the Father and of his will.

In the Old Testament, the Hebrew term *dabar* means "word." Its use in the Old Testament is fascinating, for it often seems to refer to the Word in a divine personified coming, speaking and revealing of God's will to men.

In this chapter an attempt will be made to present what

Christ as the Word

might be the Old Testament root of the New Testament teaching of the Word as being Christ, the second Person of the Godhead.

In seeking to trace the teaching of the personified Word in the Old Testament, we turn first to the creation story. It does not refer to the personified Word, except by the recurring speech of God: "And God said, Let there be . . . ." There is actually no clear reference to the personified Word until after the period covered by the Pentateuch, the first five books of Scripture. The reason seems to be that in the Pentateuch, the Mal'akh Jahweh is the Messenger of God and his mouthpiece. In the days of Samuel however, we read:

> And the LORD appeared again in Shiloh. For the LORD revealed Himself to Samuel in Shiloh by the word of the LORD. (1 Samuel 3:21 KJ II)

Here Samuel by inspiration says that Jahweh appeared to him in Shiloh and that he revealed himself by the Word of the Lord. It was in the appearance of God to Samuel that the Word came to Samuel. When the WORD spoke to Samuel, Samuel learned what the will of God was for him and the people of Israel.

Although not as clearly as in the New Testament, the Old Testament at times seems to picture "the Word of the Lord" as a divine Person of the Godhead. He appears. He comes to Samuel. He speaks.

While "the word of the Lord came to . . . " is the standard Old Testament way of introducing what God says, we suggest it might also convey the concept of the personified Word.

We read of the coming of the Word of the Lord to Samuel later in his life. This time it concerned the wayward king Saul:

> Then the word of the LORD came to Samuel saying, It grieves Me that I have set up Saul to be king. For he has turned back from following Me and has not done My commandments. And it grieved Samuel, and he cried out to the LORD all night. (1 Samuel 15:10,11 KJ II)

The Word of Jahweh said he was grieved with Saul, because Saul had stopped following him and had disobeyed him. Samuel was so grieved by the message that he prayed in anguish all night.

Here again when the Word of the Lord speaks, God is speaking. When Saul went astray, he strayed from the Word.

During the reign of David, a coming of the Word to Nathan is recorded:

> And that night the word of the LORD came to Nathan, saying, Go and tell My servant David, Thus says the LORD, shall you build Me a house for Me to dwell in? For I have not lived in any house since the day that I brought up the children out of Egypt until this day, but have walked in a tent and in a tabernacle. In all the places in which I have walked with all the children of Israel, did I speak a word with any of the tribes of Israel, whom I commanded to feed My people Israel, saying, Why do you not build Me a house of cedar? Now therefore, so shall you say to My servant David, Thus says the LORD of hosts: I took you from the sheepcote, from following the sheep, to be ruler over my people, over Israel. And I was with you wherever you went and have cut off all your enemies out of your sight, and have made you a great name like the name of the great men who are in the earth.

Moreover I will appoint a place for My people Israel and will plant them so that they may dwell in a place of their own and move no more. Neither shall the children of wickedness afflict them any more, as before. And even from the time that I commanded judges to be over My people of Israel, so I will cause you to rest from all your enemies. Also the LORD tells you that He will make you a house. And when your days are fulfilled, and you shall sleep with your fathers, I will set up your seed after you, who shall come out of your bowels. And I will make his kingdom sure. He shall build a house for My name, and I will establish the throne of his kingdom forever. I will be his Father, and he shall be My son. If he commits iniquity, I will chasten him with the rod of men, and with the stripes of the children of men. But My mercy shall not leave him, as I took it from Saul, whom I put away before you. And your house and your kingdom shall be made sure forever before you. Your throne shall be established forever. According to all these words, and according to all this vision, so Nathan spoke to David. (2 Samuel 7:4-17 KJ II)

In this section, the Lord commends David for his desire to build a temple. He then tells David that God will build David a house, that from David the Savior would be born. Here the Word serves as the spokesman for God revealing God's grace and mercy to David. In 1 Chronicles 17:3-15 the same vision is recorded.

In 2 Chronicles 12, we have another of many examples of "the Word of the Lord coming":

And when the LORD saw that they had humbled themselves, the word of the LORD came to Shemaiah, saying, They have humbled themselves. I will not destroy them, but I will give them some deliverance. And My wrath shall not be poured out on Jerusalem by the hand of Shishak. But they shall be his servants so that they may know My service, and the service of the kings of the countries. (2 Chronicles 12:7,8 KJ II)

Admittedly these passages do not prove that Old Testament believers had a knowledge of the personified Word. But they do raise the possibility.

In the book of Psalms, however, the references to the personified Word become clearer. Psalm 33 speaks of the Word as a divine Being:

> For the word of the LORD is right and true; he is faithful in all he does. The LORD loves righteousness and justice; the earth is full of his unfailing love. By the word of the LORD were the heavens made, their starry host by the breath of his mouth. (Psalm 33:4-6 NIV)

Here the Psalmist first says the Word of Jahweh is righteous and all his works are done in truth. The Word of Jahweh is holy and true and all his works reflect this. Secondly, the Psalmist says that the cosmos was made by the Word of Jahweh, and all the countless galaxies by the utterance of his voice. The Word of Jahweh is designated here as the Creator of the Universe. He is credited with participation in the work of creation.

Psalm 147 presents the personified Word in a different light:

> He sends his command to the earth; his word runs swiftly. He spreads the snow like wool and scatters the frost like ashes. He hurls down his hail like pebbles. Who can withstand his icy blast? He sends his word and melts them; he stirs up his breezes, and the waters flow.
>
> He has revealed his word to Jacob, his laws and decrees to Israel. He has done this for no other nation; they do not know his laws. Praise the LORD. (Psalm 147:15-20 NIV)

The Word here is pictured as the Messenger of Jahweh, carrying the commands of Jahweh over the earth. He is pictured as running very swiftly. Jahweh sends his Word to the earth. He sends his Word to the frigid places and melts them; he stirs them with his wind and causes the waters to flow. The Word here is presented as the bringer of spring after a hard winter. He personally makes the seasons change for the benefit of God's people.

When we gather these truths together, we see that the personified Word in the Old Testament serves as the mouth or the mouthpiece of God. In him and through him, God created the universe. The universe reflected his glory, being perfect and holy. The personified Word is a divine Person in the Godhead. He served as the divine Spokesman for God and as the Guide and Judge of God's people. There is also evident in the concept of the personified Word of the Old Testament a strong Messianic tone. It would be the Word who would take the message of God to the remotest isles of the earth where there was only the icy cold darkness and death of the winter of sin. He would carry the message of God not only to the Jews but also to the gentiles.

He would thus be the universal Word of life. Through his message the icy darkness of sin's winter would thaw and give way to the light and life of spring. In him all men would find deliverance from sin and life, strength and favor with God.

That the Old Testament did speak of a personified Word, that he was a separate person in the Godhead and that the Jews of Jesus' day were aware of this concept can also be seen by a passage from the Apocrypha, written between the time of Malachi (400 B.C.) and the coming of Christ.

In the Wisdom of Solomon the writer is speaking of the destruction of the firstborn in Egypt. He says:

> For though they disbelieved everything because of their enchantments, when the first-born were destroyed, they acknowledged that the people was God's son. For when gentle silence enveloped everything, and night was midway of her swift course, Your all-powerful word leaped from heaven, from the royal throne, a stern warrior, into the midst of the doomed land, carrying for a sharp sword your undisguised command, and stood still, and filled all things with death, and touched heaven but waited upon the earth. (The Wisdom of Solomon 18:13-16)

Here the Word is pictured as a mighty warrior, sent from the throne of heaven to destroy according to what had been foretold. He was God's divine Messenger of death to Egypt.

St. John and the Word

In the first chapter of his Gospel, the Apostle John takes the Old Testament personified Word and brings it to its climax when he declares the Word became incarnate or a human being of flesh and blood. He did not get this teaching from the New Testament Gnostics or Greeks, as some say, but from the Old Testament concept of the personified Word. In an awesome manner he speaks of the incarnation of the personified Word, saying:

In the beginning was the Word, and the Word was with God, and the Word was God. This is the One who was in the beginning with God. Through Him everything came into being and without Him nothing that exists came into being. In Him was Life, and the Life was the Light of men. The Light shines in the darkness and the darkness did not overcome it. (John 1:1-5 Ber.)

When we view the words of John in the light of the opening words of Genesis the divinity and being of the Word is beyond dispute, for Scripture declares:

In the beginning God created the heavens and the earth. (Genesis 1:1 Ber.)

Again in John we are told:

And the Word became flesh and lived among us. And we saw His glory, the glory as of the only-begotten of the Father — full of grace and truth. (John 1:14 KJ II)

The concept of the incarnate Word or Logos is very clear in the New Testament, as the above passages indicate. It is clearly stated that at the time of creation the Word was with God. Not only was the Word with God but he was God. Without him nothing was made that was made. The Word spoken of here is designated as existing from eternity, as being God, yet separate from God, as being a participant in the act of creation. John puts, as it were, the final and complete touch to the Old Testament portrait of the divine, personified Word, by saying he became flesh and dwelt among us. Not only did he become flesh and dwell among us, but he also demonstrated the fullness of the glory of God the Father. He could do this because he was the only begotten of the Father, full of divine grace and truth, who spoke as the mouthpiece of God.

In his first letter John again speaks of the personified Word having become incarnate:

> We are writing to you about the Word of Life: He was from the beginning; we have heard Him, we have seen Him with our eyes, we have looked at Him, and our hands have touched Him. Yes, the Life has been revealed and we have seen and are witnessing and are announcing to you the eternal Life who existed with the Father and has been revealed to us. We saw Him and we heard Him and are telling you, so that you too may enjoy fellowship along with us. And this fellowship of ours is with the Father and with His Son Jesus Christ. This we are writing you so that our joy may be complete. (1 John 1:1-4 Ber.)

Here John states positively that this Word was from the beginning, from eternity. He knew this to be true and so did the rest of the apostles because they had seen him, conversed with him face to face and touched him. This Word was the Word of life. The life that was in him was shown openly, namely, the eternal life which was with the Father. This life, John states, is the life we have seen and heard, and this is the life we declare to you, so that you may have fellowship with the Father and his Son, Jesus Christ. John further declares that he and the apostles were eyewitnesses to this. In this passage the divine stature of the Word is clearly shown. He is designated as Christ, the Son of God. According to the Apostle John the Word is Christ. The Word, then, is true God, the second Person of the Holy Trinity, one in essence with the Father and the

Holy Ghost. He is indeed our Savior and the Word of life for all mankind.

The book of Revelation also refers to Jesus as the Word when it records a wondrous vision granted to John on the island of Patmos. This vision brings the Bible's picture of the personified and incarnate Word to its glorious climax:

> Then I saw heaven open and a white horse appeared. Its rider is called Faithful and True; justly He judges and wages war. His eyes are like a flame of fire, and on His head are many diadems with a name inscribed which no one knows except Himself. The robe He is wearing has been dipped in blood, and the name by which He is called is The Word of God. On white horses and clothed in fine linen, white and pure, the heavenly armies follow Him. Out of His mouth issues a sharp sword with which to smite the nations. He will rule them with an iron rod, and He treads the winepress of the furious wrath of God the Almighty. On His robe and on His thigh He has His name inscribed: King of kings and Lord of lords. (Revelation 19:11-16 Ber.)

In this vision John saw heaven opened and the Lord Jesus seated upon a white charger as the Prince of heaven. The authority and power of Christ calls to mind the words of the Mal'akh in the book of Joshua:

> I now come as the Captain of the army of Jehovah! (Joshua 5:14 Gr.)

As John looks more closely, he sees that Jesus is clothed in blood-soaked clothing. This calls to mind the words of Isaiah as he beholds the triumphant Messiah-King returning from his victory over his foes.

> Who is this coming from Edom, from Bozrah, with his garments stained crimson? (Isaiah 63:1 NIV)

By his victory he won eternal life for men and assumed all power in heaven and earth. Before the assembled host of heaven, John sees that he is called by a glorious name. That name is "The Word of God."

8. GOD AND HIS PEOPLE THROUGH THE AGES

Jesus the Messiah

If one were to draw together all the truths of Old Testament Christology, volumes could be written. It is not the intention of the author to exhaust the field, for it is inexhaustible. Rather, we wish to present some basic truths concerning the Messiah which undoubtedly were known to the believers at the time of Christ. Perhaps the best way to achieve this goal is simply to write a description of the Messiah.

Although descended from King David, he would appear as a man of undistinguished parentage. He would be born in Bethlehem at a time when the Jews no longer had a Jewish king but a king from the tribe of Edom. In spite of such a background, he would be divine, a separate person in the Godhead, angels and Satan being subordinate to him. In him would reside all power for miracles, judgment, forgiveness and retention of sins. He would be the Word of God and the Wisdom of God. His wisdom would be applied to all in a public ministry. He would be despised and rejected of men and put to death by them through falsehood, torture, flogging and execution by suspension on a tree. He would be executed with criminals for man's sins and be buried in a rich man's tomb. He would rise from the grave and cover the earth with the

Christ in the
New Testament

story of his work of redemption. He would be exalted by God to rule heaven and earth and judge all mankind. In him all believers would find forgiveness and sonship with God.

In the concepts of the human-divine Savior, the Messiah or Christ, the office of Prophet, Priest and King, the Messenger or Angel of the Lord, the Servant of the Lord, the Lamb of God, the Wisdom of God, and the Word of God, one cannot honestly deny that the crucified and risen Jesus of the New Testament is the Messiah of the Old Testament as he claimed. The Apostle John makes this very plain when he says by inspiration:

> Who is such a liar as he who denies Jesus is the promised Savior? (1 John 2:22 AAT)

> Everyone who believes Jesus is the promised Savior is God's child. (1 John 5:1 AAT)

The Old Testament Believer's Concept of God

The Old Testament believer's concept of God, then, is found closely tied to the Messianic prophecies and portraits of the Old Testament. They saw God not just as a living, holy, just, divine Being, but as a God who was infinite in love, kindness, mercy and forgiveness to those who believed in the coming Messiah and followed him.

God's covenant with his people was basically a gospel covenant, one of forgiveness and salvation through the coming Messiah. As his covenant people, God's people were, however, bound by the law which in its moral aspect showed them their sin and their need for the coming Savior. In its ceremonial aspect the law depicted his suffering and death for the forgiveness of the sins of all men. In its political or civil aspect the law laid down the basic principles by which God's people were to be governed.

When God caused his people to cease to be a self-governing nation, the political law ceased to function. And when Jesus came the ceremonial law was fulfilled. Its task was done; it had nothing further to which to point God's people. It was abolished. Only the moral law, summarized in the Ten Commandments, remained binding for all people of all time. It continues to check man's sin, to convince him of sin and to show him how to lead a godly life. But the law is unable to place man into the gospel covenant relationship with God. This is only entered into by repentance and faith in the Messiah or Savior.

God was awesome and wonderful in the eyes of his people of old. He was holy and just, as we mentioned above, but he was also the ultimate in love, kindness, mercy and forgiveness to his covenant people. In him they lived with confidence and hope, for they knew that after they died they would dwell with him in his eternal kingdom of glory.

Moses spoke of this most beautifully when he said:

> Lord, Thou hast been our home in successive generations. (Psalm 90:1 Ber.)

David re-echoed this when he said:

> Surely, goodness and unfailing love shall follow me all the days of my life and I shall dwell in the house of the LORD forever. (Psalm 23:6 Ber.)

The psalmist Asaph wrote:

> Thou wilt guide me with Thy counsel, and afterward
> Thou wilt receive me to glory. Whom have I in heaven but
> Thee? And besides Thee there is none on earth whom I
> desire. Though my flesh and my heart fail, God is the
> strength of my heart and my portion for ever. (Psalm
> 73:24-26 Ber.)

God's Old Testament people knew him by several names, each having a special meaning for them. The name Jahweh (or Jehovah, as it is often pronounced) reminded them that he is a God who keeps his word. His promises and threats never fail. The name Elohim reminded them that he is the exalted, the high and mighty God. The name Adonai reminded them that he is the Lord, the King, the Ruler of all. The name Rock reminded them that he was constant, faithful and immovable, the shelter of his people in life and after life. The name Shaddai reminded them that he was almighty, as did the rare name Abhir.

God's people of the Old Testament also recognized that in the Godhead there were three distinct persons. The Old Testament speaks of "God" as divine. We have seen how it speaks of the Mal'akh as a separate divine person in the Godhead.

It also speaks of the *Ruach* — that is, the Breath or Spirit of God or the Holy Spirit — as a separate Person in the Godhead and yet divine. Some passages which point to him are: Genesis 1:2, 2 Samuel 23:2, Job 33:4, Psalm 33:6, Psalm 139:7,8, Isaiah 42:1, Isaiah 44:3, Isaiah 48:16,17, Isaiah 59:21, Isaiah 61:1, Joel 2:28,29, Zechariah 12:10.

213

The words Trinity or Triune are not used in the Old Testament, nor, for that matter, in the entire Bible. Yet the concept of three distinct Persons in one divine Essence or Godhead, co-equal in majesty and power, is used in the Old Testament. The New Testament merely clarifies this teaching. It calls the Persons, Father, Son and Holy Ghost, and more clearly defines the ways in which the Persons of the Trinity work in the salvation of mankind.

How thankful we, God's people of today, should be that the eternal Triune God so loved our sinful human race that in his Son, the Lord Jesus Christ, he offered a covenant of salvation to all. It has always been the same since the fall of man and the giving of the promise. It will remain the same to the end of time.

God's Eternal Kingdom

When God first created the earth and all its creatures everything was perfect. There was no sickness, trouble or death. Everything was in complete harmony with God and hence a holy and joyous state of life and bliss existed.

With the entry of sin into the world, the holiness and bliss of God's creation were destroyed. Vice, anger, hatred, bloodshed and evil became common on earth. Into the world's sinful existence God placed a promise and a hope. He promised to send a Savior, who would redeem man and usher in the Messianic kingdom. This Savior would restore harmony with God, deliver man from sin and bring eternal life.

God's people looked forward to this Messianic kingdom as they placed their trust in the coming Savior. They understood that it would be theirs in the life to come. With Moses they believed that God was their eternal dwelling place and with David they believed that they would dwell in the house of the Lord forever.

To preserve this belief and hope and to share it with the world, God called out from the world a people to be his own. They were God's *qahal*, his called-out assembly, his church, and they came to be known as the nation of Israel. As a nation they formed the visible church of God in the Old Testament. The Old Testament records how the true believers of Israel, whom we would call today the invisible church, had to contend for their faith. They were required by God to be faithful, even unto death. Against heathen and hypocrite they clung to the hope of the coming Savior, his redemption and the eternal glory to be found in him.

In the fullness of time God sent his Messiah into the world to atone for the sins of mankind. In him the Old Testament church gave way to the New Testament church. Circumcision gave way to baptism. The Passover gave way to Holy Communion. The ceremonial law was ended for it was fulfilled in its Lord. No longer were God's people told where and how to worship. Now in Christ they could worship anywhere in the spirit and truth of God's holy Word. No longer were they bound by the ceremonial law. They were now beyond it. It had pointed only to the redemption through the cross, the tomb and resurrection. Now on the other side of the tomb they were able to declare to the world what had taken place, that God's redemption was complete, the time of the Messianic kingdom had arrived.

As a redeemed and free people, Christ's followers in the New Testament were called by the Greek term *ecclesia*, the called-out assembly, the church. Just as was the case in the Old Testament, God had called them out of this world to be his own. Like the Old Testament believers, they also had to contend for their faith. And just as in the Old Testament they had to learn what it meant to be faithful unto death.

No longer was the church centralized in one area by a sacrificial system. It was now dependent upon the preaching of the Word in spirit and in truth and it spread over the whole earth. Wherever Christians lived they built churches and church organizations. These outward manifestations of allegiance to Christ we today call the visible church. Within this outward organization are the real believers who make up the invisible church. These people are linked together with the Old Testament believers through faith in Jesus as the Messiah, the Christ, the Savior of the world.

Jesus gave to his New Testament church the command to continue building his kingdom throughout the earth, until he comes again in glory to judge the living and the dead. At that time he will create a new heaven and a new earth in which he will live eternally with his followers. As his church carries out its Lord's command on earth, it is called the church militant, the church that battles for its Lord. When its battle is over for each believer in time and for all believers on Judgment Day, the church militant will become the church triumphant. It will be the gathering of the redeemed, the forgiven, the holy children of God from all ages.

When this final triumph day comes for God's people, they will be forever separated from sin, death and Satan. Then bliss and holiness will again reign and God's people will dwell forever in his kingdom in heaven. God promised this years ago in the Garden of Eden and throughout biblical history. He will keep his promise to us, as he always has. God's eternal kingdom is ours by faith in Christ.

May God keep each of us to this end, for Jesus' sake!

TIMELINE

As one surveys the timeline of the ever expanding picture of the coming Messiah in the Old Testament, it should be remembered that the land mass on which Israel was settled by God was very small, about 200 miles long and about 60-90 miles wide at its greatest extent. The nation was bound together by the tabernacle or temple which was the only place where sacrifices could be offered. The people were very religious. Any prophetic activity or message would become known very rapidly, since the people lived in villages and cities which had frequent contact with each other and because of the obligation for all to offer sacrifices at the temple. The messages of the prophets were thus inevitably and rapidly carried to all corners of the land. The Bible tells us of this type of transmission of news after the circumcision and naming of John the Baptist when it says in Luke 1:65:

> And fear came on all that dwelt round about them: and all these sayings were *noised* abroad through all the hill country of Judea. (KJV)

Again during the ministry of Christ we hear of this in Matthew 9:26:

> And the fame hereof went abroad into all that land. (KJV)

The various concepts of the Messiah would thus be known throughout the country, since the Bible says that all the prophets spoke of him and his coming.

THE MESSIANIC TIMELINE
The Growth of the Knowledge of the Messiah in the Old Testament

Dates	People and Footprints of the Messiah	Cumulative Portrait of the Messiah
PRE-FLOOD ERA Approx. 4000 B.C. to Approx. 2000 B.C.	Adam and Eve — the Fall into sin. God's judgment of death rests upon the human race. God gives the Protevangel, the first promise of the coming seed. He would be human, yet divine. He would suffer, die, but be victorious over Satan who had destroyed man. The Seed would reconcile God to man and end the enmity brought into being by sin. This was the initial gospel covenant of God for man.	The Seed of the Woman
POST-FLOOD ERA to end of the SOJOURN IN EGYPT Approx. 2000 B.C. to Approx. 1450 B.C.	Noah — God renewed the gospel covenant of the Seed. Shem — the ancestor of Messianic cradle or the Hebrew people. Japheth — the ancestor of the Europeans. Abraham — God renewed the promise of the Seed. Abraham is made the father of Messianic cradle or the Hebrew people. The Mal'akh Jahweh shows himself to be the guide and guardian of the Messianic people, Abraham's descendants. Melchizedek — a type of the Messiah as Priest-King.	The Seed of the Woman The Seed of Abraham The Mal'akh Jahweh, the divine Messenger of God Shiloh, the Bringer of Peace

	Isaac — a type of the Messiah. Isaac, the son of promise, the beginning of laughter or joy to the earth.	The Seed of the Woman
	Jacob — the beginner of the Hebrew people.	The Seed of Abraham
	The Mal'akh Jahweh, the protector and Lord of God's people.	The Mal'akh Jahweh, the divine Messenger of God
	The coming of Shiloh foretold. The birth of the bringer of peace, the Messiah, to be when the Judean kings ceased.	Shiloh, the Bringer of Peace
	Judah, the tribe of kings and the Messianic tribe.	The "Prophet"
EXODUS to the end of the JUDGES Approx. 1450 B.C. to Approx. 1100 B.C.	Moses — the deliverer and organizer of the Hebrew people through the Exodus.	The "Word"
	The Mal'akh Jahweh, the deliverer of his people.	The "Priest"
	The gospel covenant relationship of God with the Messianic people.	
	The coming Messiah to be the "Prophet."	
	Joshua — the establisher of the Hebrew race in the Promised Land.	
	The Mal'akh Jahweh leads his people to victory in the Promised Land.	
	Public judgment by the Mal'akh Jahweh on the Hebrew people at Bochim.	
	Samson — the deliverer or judge of the Hebrew people.	
	The Mal'akh Jahweh, God's Messenger to Samson's parents.	

Dates	People and Footprints of the Messiah	Cumulative Portrait of the Messiah
	Samuel — the Deliverer or Judge of the Hebrew people. The "Word" of God. The Messiah, "the Priest."	
UNITED KINGDOM Approx. 1100 B.C. to Approx. 975 B.C.	David — the King of the Hebrew people; the father of the family of the Messiah. The Messiah, the "King." The Messiah, the "Seed of David." Solomon — Proverbs. The Messiah, the "Wisdom" of God.	The Seed of the Woman The Seed of Abraham The Mal'akh Jahweh, the divine Messenger of God Shiloh, the Bringer of Peace The "Prophet" The "Word" The "Priest" The "King" The Seed of David The "Wisdom" of God
DIVIDED KINGDOM Northern Kingdom of Israel (Ten Tribes) Approx. 975-722 B.C. Southern Kingdom of Judah (Two Tribes) Approx. 975-606 B.C. and 586 B.C.	Isaiah — the Minstrel of the Hebrew people. The mother and birth of the Messiah. The Messiah, Root of Jesse and the Shoot out of the dry ground. The two natures of the Messiah, human and divine. The place of the Messiah's labor, Galilee. The work and triumph of the Messiah. The Ebed Jahweh, the Suffering Servant of God, the Messiah.	The Seed of the Woman The Seed of Abraham The Mal'akh Jahweh, the divine Messenger of God Shiloh, the Bringer of Peace The "Prophet" The "Word" The "Priest" The "King"

	Micah — the place of the birth of the Messiah. Jeremiah — the Messiah — the "Branch."	The Seed of David The "Wisdom" of God The Ebed Jahweh, the Suffering Servant The "Branch"
BABYLONIAN CAPTIVITY Approx. 606–536 B.C.	Daniel — the Prophet of the exile in the palace of Babylon. The Mal'akh Jahweh — the Protector of his people. The Messiah, the God-sent Stone or Rock whose kingdom would fill the earth. The glory and triumph of the Messiah in heaven.	The Seed of the Woman The Seed of Abraham The Mal'akh Jahweh, the divine Messenger of God Shiloh, the Bringer of Peace The "Prophet" The "Word" The "Priest" The "King" The Seed of David The "Wisdom" of God The Ebed Jahweh, the Suffering Servant The "Branch"
POST-BABYLONIAN CAPTIVITY to INTER-TESTAMENTAL PERIOD	Zechariah — The Mal'akh Jahweh, the Judge and Ruler of all, including Satan. The Mal'akh and the Ebed Jahweh combined in prophecy.	The Seed of the Woman The Seed of Abraham The Mal'akh Jahweh, the divine Messenger of God Shiloh, the Bringer of Peace

Dates	People and Footprints of the Messiah	Cumulative Portrait of the Messiah

Approx. 536–444 B.C.	The prophecy of the Messiah coming to his people on a donkey and bearing salvation.
	
	Malachi —
	    The designation of the Mal'akh as the Messiah.
		The "Prophet"
		The "Word"
		The "Priest"
		The "King"
		The Seed of David
		The "Wisdom" of God
		The Ebed Jahweh,
		    the Suffering Servant
		The "Branch"
		The Mal'akh Jahweh to be
		    the Messiah

BIBLIOGRAPHY

Arndt, William F. and Gingrich, Wilbur F. *A Greek - English Lexicon of the New Testament.* Chicago: University of Chicago Press, 1952.

Beck, William F. *The Holy Bible An American Translation.* New Haven, Missouri: Leader Publishing Co., 1976.

Berry, George Ricker. *A New New Testament.* Chicago: Wilcox and Follett Co., 1948.

Bewer, Julius A. *The Book of Isaiah.* Vol. II. New York, New York: Harper and Brothers Publishers, n.d.

Bible, Hebrew. New York: Hebrew Publishing Co., n.d.

Bible, New International Version. Grand Rapids, Michigan: Zondervan Bible Publishers, 1978.

Bible, The Complete, An American Translation. Chicago: University of Chicago Press, 1949.

Borland, James A. *Christ in the Old Testament.* Chicago: Moody Press, n.d.

Bouman, Rev. Walter H., Sr. *Prophecy and Fulfillment.* Translated and Adapted from an article by Dr. George Stoeckhardt in "Lehre und Wehre." XXX, XXXI. (1884-1885). n.p., n.d.

Cook, F.C., Editor. *Bible Commentary on the Old Testament.* Grand Rapids, Michigan: Baker Book House, 1969.

Cruden, Alexander. *Cruden's Complete Concordance.* Philadelphia, Pennsylvania: Universal Book and Bible House, n.d.

Cruse, Frederick Christian. *Eusebius' Ecclesiastical History.* Grand Rapids, Michigan: Guardian Press, 1976.

Edersheim, Alfred. *Old Testament Bible History.* Grand Rapids, Michigan: Wm. B. Eerdmans Publishing Company, 1969.

Frew, Robert, Editor. *Barnes on the Old Testament.* Grand Rapids 6, Michigan: Baker Book House, 1968.

Gerhardi, Ioannis. *Loci Theologici.* Vol. VIII. Lipsiae, J.C. Hinrichs, 1885 pp. 351, 366, 371, 430, 433.

Green, Jay P. *Holy Bible King James II Version.* Grand Rapids, Michigan: Associated Publisher and Authors, 1971.

Green, Jay. *The Interlinear Hebrew/Greek English Bible.* Wilmington, Delaware: Associated Publishers and Authors, 1976.

Heinisch, Dr. Paul. *History of the Old Testament.* Translated by William Heidt. Collegeville, Minnesota: The Liturgical Press, n.d.

Hengstenberg, E.W. *Christology of the Old Testament.* MacDill AFB, Florida: MacDonald Publishing Company, n.d.

Henry, Matthew. *Matthew Henry's Commentary.* New York: Fleming H. Revell Company, n.d.

Hoenecke, Adolf. *Hoenecke Dogmatik.* Vol. II. Milwaukee, Wisconsin: Northwestern Publishing House, n.d., pp. 157-161.

Honsey, Rudolph E. "The Personal Wisdom in Proverbs Eight." B.D. Thesis, St. Louis, Missouri: Concordia Seminary. June 1945.

Interlineary Hebrew English Psalter, The. New York: Harper and Brothers, n.d.

Keil, C.F. and Delitzsch, F. *Keil and Delitzsch, Commentaries on the Old Testament.* Grand Rapids, Michigan: Wm. B. Eerdmans Publishing Company, 1951.

Kretzmann, Paul E. *Popular Commentary of the Bible.* St. Louis, Missouri: Concordia Publishing House, 1923.

Langenscheidts Taschen-Wörterbücher. Switzerland: Langenscheidtsche Verlagsbuchhandlung, K.G., Berlin-Schoneberg, 1948.

Lehman, Helmut T., General Editor. *Luther's Works,* Vol. 1, 35, 40. Philadelphia and St. Louis: Muehlenberg Press and Concordia Publishing House, n.d., n.p.

Leupold, H.C. *Leupold on the Old Testament.* Grand Rapids, Michigan: Baker Book House, 1968, 1970.

Meusel, Dr. Carl. *Kirkliches Handlexikon.* Zweiter Band. Leipzig, Germany : 1889, pp. 373-375.

Mueller, Dr. John Theodore. *Christian Dogmatics. Vol. I, II, III.* St. Louis, Missouri: Concordia Publishing House, 1950.

Nestle, Eberhard, Editor. *Greek New Testament.* New York: American Bible Society, n.d.

Oehler. *Old Testament Theology.* St. Louis, Missouri: Concordia Publishing House, 1934.

Pieper, Francis. *Christian Dogmatics. Vol. I, II, III.* St. Louis, Missouri: Concordia Publishing House, 1950.

Pusey, E.B. *Pusey on the Old Testament.* Grand Rapids, Michigan: Baker Book House, 1967, 1968.

Real Encyklopedie for Protestantische Theologie and Kirche. Band XV, XVI. Leipzig, Germany : 1885, pp. 538, 15.

Sauer. Dr. Alfred von Rohr. Old Testament Theology Notes. St. Louis, Missouri: Concordia Seminary, n.p., n.d.

Spence, H.D.N. and Epell, Joseph S., Editors. *The Pulpit Commentary.* Grand Rapids, Michigan: Wm. B. Eerdmans Publishing Company, 1950.

Theologisches Wörterbuch zum Neuen Testament. Band I, II, III. Stuttgart, Germany: Verlag von W. Kohlshammer, n.p., n.d.

Thompson, Frank Charles, Editor. *The New Chain Reference Bible.* (King James Version). Indianapolis, Indiana: B.B. Kirkbride Bible Co. Inc., 1957.

Tregelles, Samuel Prideaus. *Gesenius' Hebrew and English Lexicon.* Grand Rapids, Michigan: Eerdmans Publishing Company, 1959.

Verkuyl, Gerrit, Editor-in-chief. *The Holy Bible, The New Berkeley Version in Modern English.* Grand Rapids, Michigan: Zondervan Publishing House, 1969.

Vogel, H. "The Angel of the Lord." *Wisconsin Lutheran Quarterly,* Vol. 73 (April 1976), pp. 105-118.

Walther, C.F.W. *Baieri Compendium.* Vol. II. St. Louis, Missouri: Concordia Publishing House, n.d., pp. 5, 46, 103 ff.

Young, Robert. *Young's Literal Translation of the Holy Bible.* Grand Rapids, Michigan: Baker Book House, 1956.

INDEX OF SCRIPTURE PASSAGES

The Apocrypha